A Woman's Book of Balance

ALSO BY KAREN ANDES

A Woman's Book of Power

A Woman's Book of Strength

A Woman's Book of Balance

Finding Your Physical, Spiritual,

and Emotional Center with Yoga,

Strength Training, and Dance

Karen Andes

A PERIGEE BOOK

A Perigee Book
Published by The Berkley Publishing Group
A division of Penguin Putnam Inc.
375 Hudson Street
New York, New York 10014

Copyright © 1999 by Karen Andes
Book design by Richard Oriolo
Cover design by Jill Boltin
Cover and interior photographs copyright © by Bari Williams and Blake Davis
Interior illustrations: Cynthia Brody (pages 46, 56, 62); Mandala (page 22) by Beth Susanne; all other illustrations by Karen Andes
Models: Karen Andes, Sharon Fox, and Toni Zepponi

First edition: December 1999

Published simultaneously in Canada.

The Penguin Putnam Inc. World Wide Web site address is
http://www.penguinputnam.com

Library of Congress Cataloging-in-Publication Data

Andes, Karen.
    A woman's book of balance : finding your physical, spiritual, and emotional center with yoga, strength training, and dance / Karen Andes.
        p.   cm.
    Includes bibliographical references and index.
    ISBN 0-399-52567-X (tp)
    1. Physical fitness for women.   2. Yoga, Haòha.   3. Movement education.   4. Women—Mental health.   5. Dance—India.
I. Title.

RA781/A597   1999
613.7'045—dc21   99-045745
                                                                                                    CIP

Printed in the United States of America

10 9 8 7 6 5 4 3 2 1

This book is dedicated to all
seekers of beauty, balance,
and bliss.

Contents

Part Three: Creating Internal Balance

Acknowledgments

More than any of my other books, this one was nourished by woman-power! Special thanks to my female friends for sharing your gifts, your art, your beauty, yourselves. You convince me that in the circle of women, we all grow stronger, more powerful and balanced. Special thanks to those who helped birth this project:

My two models: Toni "the Trainer" Zepponi, curly locked and leggy "Queen of the Biceps" and "Goddess of Abundance." Thank you for being the brightest light on the darkest mornings and for being so potently honest, funny and delightful.

Sharon Fox, straight-and-dark-haired gorgeous yogini and "Goddess of Balance and Bliss." Thank you for sharing your pull-out-the-stops, playful magnificence and for making this a wildly wonderful photo shoot.

Bari Williams and Blake Davis, wizards of photography . . . with the two of you on the job, I know that every shot is a composition, every detail's in place. Thank you both for making my visions become realities.

Beth Susanne, my sweet friend and longtime support, Muscle Yogini, dancer and salsa mistress, thank you for reading my early drafts on the mandala, "feeling" and then creating just the right mandala for this book.

Cynthia Brody, artist, altar-maker, writer and ("don't tell my clients I'm a belly dancer") therapist. Thank you for your soulful renditions of Shiva and two dancing goddesses featured in these pages.

A big tribal hug to my greatest teachers—the women who come to my classes (if I've left out your name, please forgive me). Special thanks to my performing temple dancers: Sandy Opsomer, Danielle Mirabella, Beth Susanne, Chris Trost, Mary O'Connor, Norma Novy, Fran Rappaport, Roshan Kaderali, Mary Swift, Elizabeth Benedict and Hilda Hattar. Continued thanks to everyone who keeps showing up: Danielle Aleco, Pamela Bouchard, Patricia Hartnett, Melanie Lamoureux, Barbara Landy, Rose Wolford, Hilda Mulhauser, Donna Simonsen, Leslie Lawton, Cynthia Brody, Carol Banquer, Dianne Morrison, Beth Greer, Mary Carol Winkler, Nancy Dew, Joan Andrews and more!

Thank you, Nautilus of Marin in San Rafael, California, for letting me work my magic in two "dance studios of my dreams."

Thanks to everyone who sends regular mail and E-mail in support of this work. Hearing from you reassures me that I'm not just doing it all for me. (Keep sending E-mail to kandes@worlddancer.com.)

Thanks to Carolena Nericcio of FatChanceBellyDance, for being such a great teacher, dancer, businesswoman, role model and friend—and for collaborating on the *WomanPower Workout* video (see "Resources" at the end of this book).

Thanks yet again to Julie Merberg, for taking time away from your main job as director of Roundtable Press in New York to be my agent because you believe in this work.

Thank you, Sheila Curry at Penguin Putnam Inc., for elegantly pulling weeds from this manuscript and publishing yet another "not just a fitness" book.

Thank you, Barbara Framm of Open Secret Bookstore in San Rafael, California, for selling your books on Indian dance just when I needed to buy them!

Thanks to Jeff Tablak and Kelly Millard of Nextron in San Jose, California, for awesome Web site construction and support.

Most special thanks to my husband, Martine, teacher and tester of patience, house healer, old-world temple builder, backside watcher and closest friend for doing all the unglamorous work that it takes to build a sacred space.

As always, my most humble thanks go to the mystery collaborator—the one who *really* comes up with all these seemingly unrelated ideas and drops enough hints until I finally figure out how to weave them together. I feel blessed that you chose me to do this work. Looks like we've wrapped up another one. Thanks for working so relentlessly this time and so fast.

Blessings,
Karen Andes

Part One

Building Balance

1 Stalking the Elusive Balance Point

The idea that our lives should be balanced is a good one, but there's a big difference between outer balance and inner balance. Outer balance fluctuates with the needs of the day and the year, and how best to maintain the life structures we have worked so hard to put into place. But within each day, no matter its mix of tasks and pleasures, we can maintain an inner balance. When we are capable of living in the moment free from the tyranny of "shoulds," free from the nagging sensation that this moment isn't right, we will have peaceful hearts.
—JOAN BORYSENKO, *A WOMAN'S BOOK OF LIFE*

I confess I'm not a master of balance. But I light my candles to the goddesses of equilibrium, proportion, harmony and poise. Maybe it's my moon in Libra that creates this fascination with balanced scales, center points, symmetry and the middle path of the Buddha. Or maybe it's maturity blossoming at last. But this lofty, intangible and slippery concept called balance has become one of the most important things in my life.

I started writing this book because I felt *out* of balance. Nothing was really wrong with me. I had no disease or handicap. But I had one big problem that stooped my posture and stole my smile. I lived in a construction site. My husband, Martine, and I had bought a "fixer upper." Three days after we moved in, we started tearing down walls to fix termite damage. The more space we cleared, the more potential we saw. Before I realized what we were in for, I agreed that we should completely rebuild the house, even though we had no plans, architect, experience, big money or even a hammer to our names. I still haven't decided if that was a moment of inspiration, insanity, colossal stupidity or surrender to a fated, cosmic plan. We romanced ourselves with visions of turning our white, sexless, stucco box into a mini Italian villa, complete with arches, round windows, antique ironwork and palm trees. Fueled by magazines, how-to books, videos and faith, we felt confident that anything we did would be an improvement. But we had no idea that our one-year project would turn into a six-year odyssey.

To put it mildly, this put a tremendous strain on our marriage, our bank account and mostly my sanity. It also quickly revealed our differences. I come from the comfortable suburbs, where if you want something done you pick up the phone and you write a check. He comes from Central America and believes that you don't pay someone good money for something you can do yourself. But we didn't know how to *do* anything. We also hadn't anticipated needing a new roof and drainage system, or raising the house three feet in the air to build a new foundation! Whenever I called contractors for bids, they never said a number less than five thousand dollars. But we were already committed—the walls were open and there was no way we could afford to pay for everything that needed to get done. So Martine set out, with some fear but mostly great enthusiasm, to study framing, stucco, wiring, plumbing, etc. Instead of furniture, we bought every power tool ever invented. What started as an overly ambitious do-it-yourself project soon snowballed into Martine's very own "hero's journey," in which he no longer seemed to be rebuilding the house, but rebuilding himself. It often seemed as if he and the house were engaged in an ongoing dialogue. The house would somehow whisper, "I need a front porch with a colonnade of arches and a barrel-vaulted ceiling" and he would study how it was done and then build it. Or it would say, "I would look much better with an old-world stucco finish," and he would tear off the old stucco, apprentice with plasterers, buy stucco mixers, dyes and stains and reproduce the old techniques—all by himself. It was impressive.

Indeed, many strange forces seemed to be at work. We often went hunting at salvage yards and auctions for architectural treasures. We bought a whole set of matching arched, dual-glazed windows, elegant old pocket doors, heavy ornate ironwork, more French doors than we knew what to do with and so many wonderful pieces—in prices we could afford and in the sizes and amounts we needed; it was as if God was saying, "Here, you have the power to heal. Have some Palladian windows and check out these doors." The excitement of finding bargains, plus the vision of what could be, was sometimes enough to keep me going.

But the reality of doing the labor and living in the present was extremely difficult. For months (which turned into years), we lived without heat or hot water, with holes in the walls where the wind and rain blew through and without drywall so all the electrical wires, plumping pipes and two-by-fours were exposed. . . . The strange part was that we actually *adapted* to living this way, the way you adapt to walking with a limp.

When we started the project, I was supportive and gung ho, mostly because I had no idea what was really involved. But it kept growing and the design kept changing. Every time Martine decided to install a window, then tear it out and move it eight inches, he felt powerful because he knew how to do this, while I discovered new depths of frustration and despair. It seemed as if it would never end. So much time went by that our friends and family stopped asking, "So how's the house coming along?" They seriously worried about our marriage and my mental health and so did I. For a while I seduced myself with the thought of how happy I'd be when it was all finished. Gradually, it dawned on me that it might never be finished, so if I wanted to be happy, I needed a Plan B.

In the movie *The Natural*, Iris, the character played by Glenn Close, says to Roy Hobbs, "I believe we have two lives—the life we learn with and the life we live with after that." The house gave me "the life I learned with." It carved wrinkles in my face, drained money like blood from my veins and cast a shadow on my spirit. I was jealous of simple things other people had, like heat, hot water, weekends. I started to feel like a prisoner of my house and a slave to the bills. I cried, I nagged, I raged at my poor husband who worked so hard. I knew that if I let myself go on this way, we'd probably get divorced and/or I'd get sick. After much contemplation, I realized—much as I hated to admit it—that no, I didn't need a finished house (or anything else from the outside) to be happy. Being happy was up to me.

So, I set out to build a sanctuary inside myself and once again turned to my movement practice, the one part of my life where I felt at peace and in control. Using the humble tools of dance, strength training and yoga, I transformed my daily workouts and classes into little prayers of gratitude. I let myself fall in love with the details: with stillness, with the surrender inside each stretch, with the transitions from one move to the next. Paying exquisitely close attention started to fill me with a deep joy and gave me compassion for the parts that were still weak, hurting or unaware. It taught me to bring love to the dark places and sit in discomfort with more grace. It also restored my smile, gave me energy and helped me return to the construction in a better state of mind.

In this book, I wanted to share my blueprint for movement bliss, both the joyful devoted spirit that drives it and the actual sacred geometry on which all of these movements are based. I've long been interested in the way various movement shapes affect the spirit and mind. My first book, *A Woman's Book of Strength*, demonstrated the straight lines and half circles that you "draw" when you perform strength-building exercises. My second book, *A Woman's Book of Power*, celebrated the four rounded shapes of "feminine" movement (the circle, figure 8, spiral and snake) that you "draw" with your body when you dance in a natural, flowing way. With this book, I wanted to present a simple movement map, "The Movement Mandala," or eight lines that spread out like spokes from the hub of a wheel, which I have been using to delineate movement space for years. The mandala is an invisible structure you "implant" in your body-mind *before* you start moving and is very useful for clarifying all forms of motion and direction, especially when you dance, do muscle work and yoga.

This shape also represents a "sacred marriage" of the linear masculine within the enveloping feminine. It's a blend of man-made straight lines (essential in construction) and the rounded, pleasing forms found in nature. On a physical level, the Movement Mandala tells you where you are or should be in space. It simplifies body position, creates safer alignment, inspires better use of the muscles, deepens stretches, creates more pleasing lines and greater sensory awareness and therefore improves balance and strength. When you align your body to these angles, your placement may feel suddenly "right" or very odd because it's hard to break bad, old movement habits. However, the mandala works for everyone.

The mandala inspires "mindful motion," a kind of feng shui (the Oriental art of placement) for the body. Feng shui determines the best position for houses (also furniture, mirrors, etc.) so that energy (and good fortune) can flow through the space. Likewise, proper alignment affects the flow of energy through the body. I can't *prove* that this is true. But proper alignment certainly affects breathing, blood flow and the amount of pressure around the organs, which hugely impacts our bodies' function.

Besides providing a map for placement, the Movement Mandala, like all mandalas, is a symbol of unity. Opposites coexist within the circle. This comes as a soothing concept in a world in which so many of us feel torn between work, family, body, emotions, spirit, possessions, intellect, creativity, money and community and tossed around by illnesses, injuries, crises, cravings, relationships and unpredictable hormones. This book won't teach you to be in perfect equilibrium with all these things at all times. But it will help you create passing moments of grace and bliss in your physical practice, which gives you the resilience to deal with those other aspects of your life.

When I speak of balance in the body, I refer to a balance of activities and the ability not to fall over—which becomes more important as we age. (Half the battle against breaking bones as we get older is won by avoiding falling down in the first place.)

In traditional fitness, getting a balance of activities is what they call cross-training. Here in the "complementary," or sacred, side of the movement arts, I call it wholeness. I personally enjoy this combination of flowing dance moves, slow, meditative strength work and yoga stretches. These need not be *your* three choices. But if you want to give your body a sensible balance of activities, you should do things that:

1. Make your heart beat faster (i.e., aerobics)

2. Make your muscles stronger (i.e., strength work) and

3. Lengthen your muscles and loosen up your joints (i.e., stretching).

Perhaps most importantly, you need to love your practice or at least love *yourself* while doing it so that you do it on a regular basis.

I'm presenting dance, muscle work and yoga in one book because I want to show the connections between them. Typically, people who lift weights sometimes don't like to dance or stretch, while dancers and yoga practitioners often shy away from strength training. But to me, they're part of a whole and when I'm overloaded in one aspect or missing another, I feel physically out of balance.

Some women pick up my books, look at the exercises and ask, "Do you really want me to *do* all these?" My answer is: Do what you want, borrow the pieces that serve you and leave the rest. Or if that's still too much, simply apply the philosophy of balance somewhere else in your life.

One of the most intriguing balance tricks you'll discover here is "dynamic tension," or pulling in two or more directions at one time. This is not only a potent lesson in physics and the power of concentration (you'll be amazed at your balance when you do this), it's also the perfect metaphor for modern life. Who hasn't been pulled in many directions at once? What a relief to know that you don't have to feel bad about this. In fact, it's useful; you *have* to use opposing forces or you'll fall over.

Women *need* a physical practice. It's our best medicine for slaying the dragons of negativity, relieving stress or restoring balance when our hormones make us feel crazy. A movement practice helps us radiate in our full glory and endure when necessary. It offers us a temple within ourselves, a sanctuary where we can find comfort, pleasure and balance, no matter what's happening outside.

Balance: What It Is and Isn't

Balance is real and ideal, perfection within imperfection, the Promised Land, the philosopher's stone, the Holy Grail, that thing we seek. Even in the mundane, it glistens. Oh, to have the bills paid with money to spare, the house in order, marital harmony, the children growing strong, the body alive, centered and well-rested. Ah, to lose the shackles around our souls!

Whenever I would mention that I was writing a book about balance, people would say, "Oh, I need that." We all know we need it and shouldn't stay out of it for long. But it seems that there are always things in the way. Why is balance so elusive—and yet so important?

Balance is a force, like gravity. When that force gets wound too tight in one direction, it unwinds with a sometimes terrible intensity. That's the dark side of balance but a necessary part of the picture. Earth creates balance this way with tidal waves, tornadoes, earthquakes, firestorms, floods and droughts. Individuals have natural disasters, too, in the form of accidents, illnesses, unemployment, divorce, homelessness, and so on. But a big balance shift can be benevolent when, after the shock wears off, it sets our priorities straight. It's certainly better to live in balance for longer periods of time than to wait for crises to set things right—but that's not always possible.

Of course, living in balance in a modern world, which is so often *out* of balance, seems like a tall order. Almost everyone I know lives at a somewhat frantic pace. That's why we need lots of simple balance remedies. Deep breaths, belly laughs, human touch, telling the truth, a good meal, a cup of tea or getting a good night's sleep can all set us right again. The important thing to know about balance is that it changes every day, in the same way that our center of gravity shifts when we move. We have to achieve it in different ways all the time. What worked yesterday probably won't work today. What worked for me might not work for you.

To create an *enduring* type of balance, we need to go deeper and positively affect our body's chemistry with benevolent types of exercise, thought patterns, food and hormones (which I'll discuss in chapters 8 and 9). Beyond those remedies, we need to create a deeper solidity in ourselves. We need purpose, to feel that even our humblest acts have meaning and that we are connected to spirit and to others. When we build these things into our daily practices, they begin to ripple out and affect other areas of our lives.

Why Women Need Balance

Women need balance because, as much as it might scare us, we long to express our soul's beauty and purpose in the world and we need to feel supported enough to do so. If we're not welcomed, invited and appreciated, we may withdraw. If embraced, encouraged and given permission, we unlock our hidden treasures.

We need balance because by the time we hit middle age, some of our "juice" has been sucked dry and our adrenaline spent. We need balance so we can once again find the nectar of sweetness inside us—and use it as lovingly, sparingly and outrageously as we want.

We need balance because we may have been everything to everyone and want time to be everything to ourselves.

We need balance because throughout most of our lives we experience estrogen-testosterone highs and progesterone lows, and somewhere within our chemical mix there is a woman who is greater than the sum of her hormones.

We need balance because, as we get older, if we don't keep our bones healthy with right movement and food, we can fall over, crumble and break.

We need balance because many of us are a little damaged from the spin cycle of food deprivation, feast, guilt and exercise addiction that we have put ourselves through and need to satisfy our hunger for harmony.

We need balance because we love to adorn our beauty but often, alone in the mirror, judge ourselves unworthy—however, there is not a woman on the planet who doesn't possess the tools for total radiance.

We need balance because age often looms like a shadow instead of a golden future.

We need balance because we spend too much time in worry and not enough in bliss.

2   Everyday Bliss

If you spend time sensitizing yourself to the subtle currents of your own energy and to the life that surrounds you, your sense of reality will expand. . . . When love is applied to that process, the world begins to unfold its gifts. —LOREN CRUDEN, *THE SPIRIT OF PLACE*

This book is about movement bliss, an everyday type of ecstasy you can enjoy between going to work and doing chores. Little raptures have the power to melt frustrations, refresh your body and mind and lift you over the threshold of "flat reality"—beyond the land of taxes, dust bunnies, chaos and tedium and into a shimmering, radiant world, which is just as real if you choose to see it. Simple practices like yoga, dance and even muscle work can supply this rapture. Dance-movement celebrates the spirit and quiets a worrying mind. Yoga teaches the power of stillness and helps rebalance hormones. Strength work solidifies not only muscles and bones, but also a sense of self. These, of course, aren't the only ways in through the gates. Meditation, chanting, singing, love-making and many other activities can inspire bliss. There are, as the Sufis say, a thousand ways to pray. But these are some of my ways.

    Experiencing movement bliss doesn't take years of practice or even a very fit body. You don't need perfect technique—although strong technique and a strong body can enhance your self-expression and heighten your experience. You need an open mind, a willingness to use the same type of magic that helps you make music instead of noise, write poetry instead of mere words, cook feasts instead of food, make love instead of having sex. In the movement arts, this comes from noticing the details of breath and posture and finding significance in the subtleties.

Cultivating such a mindful and loving movement practice is especially important during middle age because it can ground our bodies and clear our minds during an odd time of our lives when we feel perhaps most full of contradictions. I don't know about you but I feel gravity tug my body closer to the earth just as my spirit is starting to soar. I feel my wisdom gathering at last just as my "memory fog" rolls in and I often forget what I know! I'm starting to feel solid in my self just as I realize that nothing is solid—especially this person called "I." I have sometimes felt confident, hopeful, content, enraged, depressed, overwhelmed and overjoyed all within a matter of minutes, especially when fueled by fluctuating hormones. Returning to my inner temple through this spiritual movement practice always helps me feel more balanced no matter what's going on. And it gives me a spark, a radiance, as if I'm walking around with a wonderful secret. It's all-around good medicine for middle-aged women.

I recently did a search on the World Wide Web on "middle-aged women" and found reams of information on mental illness, memory loss, menopause, hormone replacement therapy, cancer and heart disease—and an alarming study showing that large numbers of women between ages forty and fifty-five are too weak to carry grocery bags.[1] But there was nothing, at least on that day in cyber space, that celebrated the "chispa"—the spark, elegance and spirit of women. Yes, we need to know how to avoid health problems. But we also need more information on how to shine from within, how to cultivate a luminous, timeless sense of beauty in ourselves and the world around us, because this is just as critical to our health!

These practices can heighten our physical and spiritual beauty and teach us to channel our energies wisely. But before we move on to the practices, we'll look at some luminous women from history to see what we can learn from them.

---

1. www.womenconnect.com/info/health/oct1497a_hlt.htm

Yoginis, Dakinis and Devadasis

Most people simply allow the energy to churn a cauldron of chaotic thoughts and emotions or dissipate the energy in a superficial pursuit of pleasure, but a yogi or yogini consciously accumulates and then directs it for specified purposes.
—MIRANDA SHAW, *PASSIONATE ENLIGHTENMENT*

The dakini represents the ever-changing flow of energy with which the yogic practitioner must work in order to become realized. She may appear as a human being, as a goddess— either peaceful or wrathful—or she may be perceived as the general play of energy in the phenomenal world. —TSULTRIM ALLIONE, *THE DAKINI PRINCIPLE*

When the devadasis danced in the temple, their dance itself was considered a form of love-making, a sensuous celebration of their union with the Beloved. In essence, their dance was the dance of love. At the same time, it was also a form of storytelling.
—JALAJA BONHEIM, *APHRODITE'S DAUGHTERS*

Goddesses were the inspiration for *A Woman's Book of Power.* The muses of this book are yoginis, dakinis and devadasis. All were "priestesses" skilled in ritual, temple service and the movement arts. All come from the Hindu, Tibetan Buddhist and Tantric traditions. (Tantra refers to esoteric and often sexual wisdom from both Hindu and Buddhist cultures.) All were considered "illumined" women, part human and part goddess. In the Tantric tradition, there's no clear distinction between humans and deities. It was believed that one could possess qualities of both and, based on the seriousness of one's devotional practice, ascend a kind of spiritual ladder and earn increased stature in the deity realm.

Yoginis, dakinis and devadasis were created out of both a religion and a culture and were considered to live on the earth and in the spirit realm. These women captured my attention because they sought union with the divine *through* intense physical training that combined yoga, dance, meditation, cleansing, diet and even ritual lovemaking. Their whole lives were devoted to embodying spirit, the power of "Shakti" energy—the divine feminine principle of motion and emptiness, thought to be the ultimate creative force through which all consciousness and life manifests. They would use their womanly beauty and exquisite movements to train their minds, hone their bodies and focus their spirits on God, so that they might entice others into an awareness of the God and "Buddha-nature" within everyone. They could also be messengers of "fierce compassion" (especially the dakinis) and practice what we might now call "tough love." Sudden loss or upset was thought to be the work of yoginis and dakinis, shaking people free from illusions that prevented them from knowing God.

Because the terms *yogini, dakini* and *devadasi* could define novices, masters and everything in between, those of us who choose to emulate them can borrow these words without feeling too presumptuous about it. If nothing else, we can simply borrow their *spirit* and use it to add meaning and bliss to our daily movement prayers.

As you read about these female power-spirits, it's best to use them as the practitioners of Tantra used them. Think of them in three stages:[2]

First, invoke and visualize these elegant women-spirits in front of you. See their beautiful faces; their strong, lithe and graceful bodies; their colorful silken clothing and their abundant jewels. Smell their sandalwood perfume and the jasmine in their hair.

Next, especially as you practice your movement arts, take them *inside* you. Feel their graceful beauty pulsing under your skin. Let them glide through your muscles, blood, nerves and breath. Let them inhabit and heal you.

Finally, blend your energy with theirs. Become an alchemical cocktail, half you, half priestess or goddess. This is especially good when the burden of "flat reality" becomes too much to bear—surrender to their presence. Let them lead you back to bliss and, when you are renewed, share that bliss with others.

Yoginis were female yogis, beautiful young maidens, serious seekers of spiritual wisdom and often the center of sacred, sometimes sexual rituals. One of their first and ongoing tasks was to master their senses. By practicing yoga, they learned when to put their minds completely into their sensations and when to send their minds elsewhere. This training made them stronger and taught them how to use their energy for situations that served a higher purpose—and not waste it. Everything in the yoginis' life was geared to reminding others how to awaken to God, Buddha or the Divine.

Adorned with crowns, necklaces, bracelets, belts and ankle bells, the sometimes-naked yoginis would perform beautiful yoga postures and elegant hand gestures called *mudras*. Yoginis were regarded as "wisdom goddesses" sent from the void and created from the "wavicles" (the combination of particles and waves) stirred up by the goddess Kali.[3] (Kali is the fierce-looking goddess with bulging eyes and tongue who wears a necklace of severed heads and a belt of sev-

2. In Snow, Kimberly, *Keys to the Open Gate: A Woman's Spirituality Sourcebook*. Chapter by Tsultrim Allione (Berkeley, CA: Conari Press, 1994), 154.
3. http://clix.net/5thworld/no-osphere/3e/divlib/ttyogini.html

ered arms. Devotees of Kali say that when you love such a fierce one as Kali as your mother, then you fear nothing, your heart melts and opens.) As Kali's daughters, they carried crescent-bladed knives so that, when necessary, they could symbolically cut away people's delusions and self-limiting beliefs with one expert slice, with the compassionate purpose of turning their thoughts to God.

Yoginis even had their own how-to manual. In the fourteenth century, the *Yogini Tantras* was published in India; it detailed all the ways yoginis should worship and be worshiped. Among other things, this described sexual rituals, in which they were allowed to have sex with anyone they desired (except for their sons) and had the option of sending their minds elsewhere or could thoroughly enjoy it. Participating in sexual rituals was considered very shocking, especially back then, and broke the moral codes in India at the time. But these rituals demonstrated the special status society granted the yoginis. They were also allowed to speak their minds, get an education and marry out of their social class.

In pictures and in statuary, yoginis were often depicted as sensual women with full, round breasts; curved, feminine hips (often wrapped in ornate belts with tassels and bells) and sometimes draped in or sitting on antelope and tiger skins, said to represent their comfort in the realm of spirit and their expertise in meditation.[4] They wore jewels made of bones (to represent human essence when flesh is stripped away) and garlands of flowers in their hair (to represent the blossoming of spirit). In ritual, they would pour negativity into bowls made from human skulls and then, using their Shakti energy, transform that negativity into blissful nectar. In ceremony, a yogini would always drink first from the skull cup before offering it to others.

Perhaps you have felt the yogini's blade slice through your life at times or have been the one who does the slicing. Perhaps you have used your beauty or the beauty around you to connect with the divine. Perhaps you have learned from your yoga practice when to redirect your mind to tolerate minor discomforts, or when to embrace every sensation. Perhaps you are learning how to master your energy so that you don't waste it but pour it into the things that most serve your connection with spirit.

Dakinis were older and wiser yoginis, with more pronounced dark and light sides. Although their demon-nature was more ferocious than the yoginis', their Buddha-nature was supposedly more evolved. Dakinis were depicted as

---

4. Shaw, Miranda *Passionate Enlightenment: Women in Tantric Buddhism* (Princeton University Press, Princeton, NJ, 1994), 38.

beautiful women and old hags. In Tantric literature the words *dakini* and *yogini* were often used interchangeably because dakinis were both accomplished yoga practitioners and dancers. However, for simplicity's sake, we'll keep them separate here.

Dakinis were thought to fly naked through the highest levels of reality and therefore were called "sky-dancing women." These "queens of space" represented those who had successfully freed themselves from the burden of worldly attachments. They were enlightened because they had come to understand the emptiness within all things—yet they still danced through the sky in ecstasy, embracing life.

In the Tantric tradition, it was believed that in order for men to advance spiritually they had to seek out, worship, embrace and adore dakinis because they represented the highest manifestation of feminine spiritual power. Dakinis were regarded as "strikingly independent women who at times [could] take a proud, condescending stance toward men and at others, cooperate with men in dynamic religious partnerships. When they join forces with men, the women become spiritual allies and esteemed teachers, mystical companions and bestowers of magical powers and enlightenment. Men are portrayed not as dominators of women but as supplicants, lovers and spiritual sons and brothers. . . . A woman did not need male approval to participate or advance in Tantric circles; however, a man's progress in Tantra is marked by stages in his relationships with women. The proper homage to women is a prerequisite to his enlightenment."[5]

If one did not honor dakinis (or the power of Shakti, the feminine force), these sky-dancing women would supposedly switch out of their enticing angel guises and suddenly become flesh-eating demons! Both the beautiful and the ferocious dakinis appear throughout the *Tibetan Book of the Dead* to guide the newly dead through different parts of the journey after death. In the *Tibetan Book of the Dead,* they're known as "Dharma" or "Truth Dakinis," with one all-consuming mission—to slice through complacency using whatever means necessary and, like the yoginis, lead people back to God, by either seducing or scaring them.

It was believed that dakinis only made one major appearance in a person's life (yet appeared several times in the afterlife). If the dakini was unable to awaken someone, through either love or fear, it was believed they wouldn't call again and would let the person suffer.

5. Ibid., 37.

But dakinis were not just considered temperamental deitie□
will. They were thought to represent an aspect of our own hum□
with exaggerated "light" and "dark" sides to get their point acr□
Allione, an American Tibetan Buddhist nun, writes:

"Everyone has the possibility of becoming a Buddha or dakini ╴╴ post.
We could have little gaps in the claustrophobic game of dualism and clarity
could shine through. Therefore, even an ordinary, 'unenlightened' woman or
situation could suddenly manifest as the dakini. The world is not as solid as we
think it is, and the more we are open to the gaps, the more wisdom can shine
through and the more the play of the dakini energy can be experienced."[6]

Like the yoginis, dakinis often danced naked or adorned themselves with
hip belts and jewelry made of bones to show essence stripped to the bone, but
they also danced with rainbow-colored veils to "stir the wind" of stagnation.
To entice, they wore sweet perfumes and flowers, carried essences of herbs,
sang and chanted prayers, danced, performed mudras, carried a torch of heavenly white light and sometimes bestowed blessings and good fortune on others.
But to shock, they wielded swords (bigger than the yoginis' knives) to cut people free from old entrapments, and they often devoured the bodies they killed.

Perhaps you have experienced those gaps in reality when wisdom has
shone through, and felt a dakini fly through your life, stirring the winds of stagnation or cutting you free from illusion. Perhaps *you* have danced in the sky in
your dreams or wielded a blade and been a dakini for someone else.

Devadasis (also called *maharis*) were real women who danced in and
around Hindu temples to make offerings to the gods. They were regarded as
brides of the temple god and, in fact, were married to that deity in a sacred
wedding ritual, much the same way Catholic nuns are wed to Jesus. Devadasis
honored the deity by dancing either alone (as if for their "husband") or in front
of an audience. Sometimes they even traveled into villages like missionaries,
where they would dance the stories of gods and goddesses or simply embody
the divine spirit with their dancing. They also served in humble ways: bathing,
adorning, "feeding" and worshiping statues and other holy figures of temple
deities. However, even the humblest aspect of a dancer's life was geared to
expressing a longing for union with God.

People watched these dancers not only to learn the stories of gods and goddesses but also to *feel* their ecstasy, for the dances transported the dancers and

6. Snow, Kimberly, *Keys to the Open Gate*. Chapter by Tsultrim Allione, 158.

the audience out of normal reality and into the realm of the gods. Because of this, dancers were considered "enlightened beings" and symbols of good fortune. No celebration was complete, in fact, without the presence of the devadasis.

Temple dancing in India goes back more than two thousand years. For much of that time, becoming a devadasi was the only way a girl could escape poverty and get an education—not only in dance, music and gesture but also in philosophy, conversation and the mystical arts. Many low and high caste families gave their daughters (sometimes as young as seven) to the temples for dance training. A young dancer would usually study for about seven years before her first official public dance performance—often done for a king.

Although the training was rigorous (they'd get up before dawn and often dance for hours), the dancers often led independent, even comfortable lives. During the height of this tradition (between the sixth and thirteenth centuries A.D.), some temples employed, housed and fed as many as four hundred dancers. Poorer temples had just a few. Some dancers earned salaries, some just their keep. Some had houses on the grounds, male companions and children—and would train their daughters to become dancers and their sons to become temple musicians. Others had no possessions and were celibate.[7]

Devadasis danced what are now considered the classical Indian dance styles: Bharata Natyam from the south, Odissi from the east and Kathak from the north. Most of these styles have been preserved and are danced in much the same way today as they were back then. These classical Indian dances are perhaps the most exquisitely beautiful and sophisticated dance styles ever created—and the hardest to master, full of extremely complex, rhythmic footwork, highly detailed body postures, over a hundred hand gestures, plus various head, neck, nostril, eye and eyebrow positions. Dancers took years just to master the basics.

Dancers had to be fluent in both the feminine qualities (called *lasya*), with curved body positions and soft, rounded movements, and the masculine qualities (called *tandava*), with quick moves and sharp lines. Accomplished devadasis would then dance themselves and their observers into a trance, and they did this *through technique!* In other words, they didn't just hear (or sing) the music, surrender to the flow and improvise, as many of us in the west do today. To them, highly deliberate steps and body positions provided *the* path to divine consciousness because they believed specific postures and rhythms represented ideal forms, which represented the perfection of the universe. Some improvisation was allowed but it was always done *within* the technique.

---

7. Devi, Ragini, *Dance Dialects of India* (Delhi, India: Motilal Banarsidass Publishers, 2nd ed., 1990), 47.

Some ancient texts describe, in detail, various devadasi traditions. The *Natya Shastra* (or "Science of Dance-Drama"), which scholars believe was written sometime between A.D. 200 and 800, gives intricate details on postures and choreography, as well as information on how to stage dance dramas, choose a temple site and perform ceremonies. Chidambaram, one of the most famous temples in the eastern Indian state of Orissa, is decorated with statues that depict the 108 "rhythmic units of dance" (called *karanas*) described in the *Natya Shastra*. Many other temples, most notably Jagannath, Lingaraj and Konarak, are also covered with statues of sacred dancers.

Another book, the *Abhinaya Darpana* ("Mirror of Gesture"), written in the fourteenth century, was more like a dancer's book of etiquette—some of it quite severe. According to this text, a girl could pretty much forget a successful temple dance career if she had "pale eyes like a flower, scanty hair, thick lips, pendant breasts, very thin or stout figure, very tall or short stature, bad voice or humped [*sic*] back."[8] On the other hand, she'd succeed if she was "lovely, young, with full round breasts, self-confident, charming, agreeable, dexterous in handling the critical passages, skilled in steps and rhythms, quite at home on the stage, expert in posing hands and body, graceful in gesture with wide open eyes, able to follow song, instruments and rhythm, . . . adorned with costly jewels and had a charming lotus face."[9] She also needed to know how to stay within her boundaries when dancing and be "conversant in the art of whirling."[10]

The devadasis were indeed beautiful to look at. Early statues show them, like yoginis and dakinis, half or fully naked and covered with jewels. Some scholars attribute their nakedness to a shortage of cloth. I disagree! These women appear much too divinely erotic and proud of their naked bodies to represent a cloth shortage—yet there's also a purity about them. These days modesty is considered an important part of the dancer's character. Perhaps it was back then, too, but it's harder for our modern minds to see modesty and eroticism existing at the same time.

Eventually, though, dancers wore brightly colored saris, or leggings and tops or dresses. They also covered themselves in jewels to bring awareness of God to the tiniest places and "mimicked the sound of the universe" through the jangling of bangles and bells. Even the act of dressing was considered a form of prayer. Devadasis also wore a bindi, the sacred forehead dot (also called a *tilak*) made of sandalwood paste or vermilion (now you can buy them in packages

---

8. Kishore, B. R., *Dances of India* (New Delhi, India: Diamond Pocket Books, 1988), 34.
9. Ibid, 33.
10. Avtar, Ram, *Indian Dances, History and Development* (New Delhi, India: Pankaj Publications, 1984), 34.

and stick them on). This famous mark has many meanings. Because it stimulates and decorates the third eye, it's worn as a sign of respect to the "inner deity" and therefore shows a willingness to overcome the ego. Monks also wear the spot for this reason, as do married women because marriage and childbirth are considered the ultimate selfless acts.[11] Bindis are also worn as signs of happiness and good fortune.

Although a dancer's beauty and ability were valued highly, her inner life was even more important. Mrinalini Sarabhai, a modern Bharata Natyam dancer, writes of the tradition:

"All Indian art has to have a deep foundation of study and intuition and devotion. Only with this foundation can the artist feel a sense of achievement. Only then, can the dancer sing of God or man. Only then, can she tell the story of a king or peasant. Only then, can she enlighten the audience through conflict and awareness."[12]

The devadasi tradition went through many hard times throughout history, fading away and starting up again. But the toughest time came when the British arrived in India in the nineteenth century. The Victorian English couldn't understand how sensual dance and holiness could coexist in a sacred setting. So they branded the devadasis as "temple prostitutes," although they were not. It's true that some devadasis followed the yogini tradition and made love to whomever they pleased, because they believed that lovemaking helped them strengthen their Shakti energy. Men lucky enough to make love with a devadasi also believed they'd become gods in a devadasi's embrace. But the devadasis had never been regarded as whores. When Anglican missionaries set out to purify the culture, one of the first things they did was force the dancers out of the temples. Suddenly, these dancers with a two-thousand-year-old tradition were stripped of their life's purpose and dumped on the streets, many with children to support. Some had no choice *but* to become prostitutes, which of course fed the prejudice against them.

Perhaps the saddest outcome of all this was the way the British planted shame in the Indian people themselves, who then turned dance—in a land where the god Shiva is worshiped as the dancer at the center of the universe—into a sin. They also turned it into a crime. On January 27, 1948, after India gained independence, *Indian,* anti-Hindu reformers passed the Devadasi Act, which officially made temple dancing illegal. Women found "performing, per-

11. www.rbhatnagar.ececs.uc.edu:8080/srh_home/1996_9msg00176.html
12. Sarabhai, Mrinalini, *Understanding Bharata Natyam* (Gujarat, India: Darpana Publications, 6th ed., 1996), 3.

mitting or abetting" temple dance were punished with six months' imprisonment, were publicly branded as prostitutes and were not permitted to enter into a legal marriage.[13] From that day forward, there was no more dancing in the temples.

Dance then moved out of the temples and into dance academies and community halls and became more secular entertainment. A few rugged temple dancers kept the sacred tradition alive in secret but did so at their own peril. The Devadasi Act still stands in the Indian law books, although according to an article in *Hinduism Today,* "people have forgotten that it exists and . . . believe that dance and music depicting some face of God, belongs in the temple once again."[14]

As I write this, dance has not yet returned to the temples in India, except in scattered festivals and workshops, although it has slowly started moving back into spiritual and religious services, especially in the United States and Europe. More importantly, dance has once again started to serve a sacred purpose in both private lives and public service as more of us are dancing our way back to the temple within ourselves.

13. Ibid., 2–3.
14. www.spiritweb.org/HinduismToday/94-01-Devadasis_Part_IV.html, 4.

3 Mandala

A mandala, the Sanskrit word for circle, is a concrete symbol of its creator's absorption into a sacred center. In its most elevated form, the sacred circle mirrors an illumined state of consciousness through a symbolic pattern, making the invisible, visible.
—JUDITH CORNELL, *MANDALA*

The mandala provides a blueprint of enlightened vision. Ordinarily, each person experiences a world that reflects her cultural background, personal neuroses and attachments, and habitual patterns of thought and behavior (known as karma). Meditation on a mandala replaces the habitually dulled way of seeing the world with a bright, crystalline view of radiant colors, beautiful forms, and divine images and sounds.
—MIRANDA SHAW, *PASSIONATE ENLIGHTENMENT*

Throughout the world, builders have long used the geometry of a square within a circle, otherwise called a mandala, as a blueprint for constructing temples, mosques and other sacred spaces. Ancient Hindu builders, in fact, not only used this design as a floor plan, they also ritually drew a mandala on the earth to invoke the *spirit* of the temple before laying the first stone. This ritual was considered just as important as a foundation was for the integrity of the building itself.

This same mandala also works as a "movement map." I didn't choose this shape because it's trendy or spiritual or because ancient builders used it. It chose me. I've been doodling this design for so many years and using it to delineate movement space, I can't say how long it's been with me. (I had this shape tattooed on my back in the mid 1980s. Back then I called it "the lines of force.") Perhaps it's just a "lucky" accident that this universal form, which has appeared in magnificent works of art and architecture throughout history, complements both the structure and the spirit of the movements I'm presenting here.

I've often assumed that many dancers, yoginis and the like frame their movements within these specific angles and directions—and some do. But when I refer to them in classes I often receive blank stares. So, I figured it was time for a full explanation of the "Movement Mandala." But first, some history.

A Brief History of the Mandala

Mandala is the Sanskrit word for "circle." More precisely, it means "container of spirit." Mandalas are womb-like structures, which envelop other circles, squares, triangles, deities and all sorts of shapes and designs. The most common mandala, however, is based on the square within the circle because these two shapes represent a marriage of the round and straight, the feminine and masculine, spirit and matter, ideal and real. Many other sacred geometric forms—the triangle, crescent, cross, pyramid, oval, pentagram and six-pointed Star of David—grow from these two shapes. The circle represents nature and the female principle—all that is continuous, soft and flowing. It's the sun, the moon, the earth, all the orbits of planets and stars and the physical bodies of most living things. The square or line represents things man-made, with beginnings and endings that are sharp and abrupt, yet familiar and dependable, "fair and square." Four corners create a grounded base, solidity, substance. Together, the square and the circle wed the male and female principles into one complete form.

A mandala is an expression of the infinite, which speaks directly to the right brain—the hemisphere that recognizes geometric forms, patterns, movement and the *relationships* among them. This side of the brain also appreciates harmony of all sorts: the placement of objects, movements, rhythms and musical notes. It appreciates the way they resonate with each other—and notices when they don't. In less than a second, the right brain can perceive a mandala and the wholeness it represents. The left, logical brain, which admires precision and mathematical order, also appreciates the mandala, although it takes longer for this side of the brain to understand why.

Because the mandala is a framework that folds around everything inside it, it's the ultimate symbol of integration. Opposites can live inside it in peace. Even antagonists can be knit into one design. It's a virtual logo for nondualistic thinking.

Mandalas aren't just man-made structures. Snowflakes, spiderwebs, beetle backs, flowers, flower stems, sand dollars, starfish, sea anemones and things too numerous to list are all mandalas. So are the cycles of the seasons, the sun, moon and stars. Even our menstrual cycles, when mapped through all their phases, become mandalas. Therefore, it's easy to understand how the mandala became a recurring theme in artwork and design throughout the world. Every civilized culture, including the Hindus, Tibetans, Chinese, Aztecs, Mayans, American Indians, Egyptians, Northern Europeans and Celts, created mandalas. Aztecs and Mayans used them to track time on their calendars. Buddhists and American Indians used them to represent "the Wheel of Life" or "Medicine Wheel." Tibetan Buddhist monks and Navajo Indians, in particular, both ritually created and destroyed mandalas made of colored sand or stone, which were used as symbols of impermanence, initiation and healing. Druids built Stonehenge in the shape of a mandala and used this geometric design to chart the movement of the stars. Feng shui practitioners based their harmonious designs on an eight-pointed mandala called a *pa kua*. Mandalas even made an appearance in Christian art and architecture. The stained-glass rose windows in Notre Dame and Chartres are mandala-inspired as well.

Perhaps the mandala is so universal because it represents a microcosm of life itself, a blending of inner and outer worlds. The outer edge of the circle frames, protects and lends significance to everything it contains. In many Buddhist mandalas, deities dance in this heavenly outer wheel and therefore represent perfect beings who have overcome the three illusions—lust, ignorance and hatred—that keep humans from experiencing a state of Nirvana. The inner wheel often contains specific information on how to overcome these illusions.

The nucleus of the mandala is the power spot, a throne, a perch and lookout, often reserved for a deity. In our own personal mandalas, however, this is *our* spot. *We* become that deity. We sit, stand, dance, draw or simply observe from the center of our own universe. From that center, lines radiate out to infinity. But they also lead the other way, from the cosmos back to us.

Psychologist Carl Jung discovered that people often spontaneously draw mandalas. He believed that we're all inclined to frame our experiences inside a circle, and that doing this helps us to reshape our painful and random experiences into rich patterns and beautiful forms.

People have long used mandalas as meditation tools, not simply to gaze at a pretty design and "space out." The mandala helps us overcome our illusions that the world is merely a drab and frightening place. The mandala is a model for a much more beautiful reality, which can teach us to see grace at the center of a complex, often frightening outer world. When we enter the spirit of the mandala, we come to the place where holy beings live, where the ideal is real, where we ourselves are transformed from everyday creatures with worries and problems into radiant beings! We enter a "Buddha dwelling," the place inside us in which the whole universe dwells.

The mandala brings necessary medicine to the modern world, where buildings are squat, ugly and devoid of lust, where pop music numbs the senses, where it's easy to get caught up in the rat race and forget about God, where art represents chaos more often than beauty and where ritualized movement often looks as appealing as an assembly line. Somewhere along the way, we lost our connection to the sacred, but we can use the mandala to find our way back.

Wisdom of the Medicine Wheel: The Four Directions

Traveling the Medicine Wheel is the journey of the soul exploring all aspects of life. There is no duality on the wheel. The further you go into understanding of the East, the deeper is your cognition of the West. Balance then is not compromise, it is completeness. . . . Imbalance comes from boxing yourself into one spot on the wheel. . . .

The Medicine Wheel is a place to form intentions, to pray. When you construct a Medicine Wheel, do it in a sacred manner with right intention, centeredness and attention. Attention, simple as it sounds, takes practice. . . . Another essential ingredient is gratitude. . . . When you forget to honor, you forget to love, and you lose touch with your own soul. Gratitude is a state of grace. It clears and strengthens you. When you live in a sacred way, you are open to power and grateful for life. —LOREN CRUDEN, *THE SPIRIT OF PLACE*

The Medicine Wheel is the symbol of time and a primer for evolving souls, since it spells out the stages of life we must go through in order to complete a full cycle—plus specific instructions about how to live according to where we are on the wheel. It's both a mandala and a simple compass, with four cardinal directions—north, south, east and west—plus four lesser, diagonal directions. The Medicine Wheel also contains two *more* directions on a vertical axis, pointing to Father Sky above and Mother Earth below.

As the wheel turns, each revolution brings new lessons, new insights and revelations. The wheel, of course, is always turning but has many different tempos. We experience a full revolution every minute, hour, day, week, month, year, and so on. So we're always in a state of turning and re-turning. Yet the directions still inform us, no matter if the revolution is small or vast.

North is the pole star, the fixed point, the place of orientation and the place to begin. It's the direction of our elders and ancestors and where wisdom lies. North is winter white, the frozen seed, the peaceful sleep where souls retreat between days and lifetimes, where visions slip into the dark cradle of the unconscious. Potential gathers force here while dreams deliver answers. The north is midnight, both beginning and end, a time to slow, take notice of the passing, take care of one's soul and cleanse past hurts and pains. It's the place of death and rebirth. Here busy-ness ends and stillness rules.

East is the yellow dawn with dew on the grass, the sun launching over the horizon, the first moment of awakening, hunger in the belly, seedlings kicking out of their pods. It's a time to shake off weariness, roam, hunt, eat and nurture the fire that rises inside. The spirit of the east is clean, new and moist as a spring rain. Intention is pure, potential is unrealized, yet inspiration is high. It's the age of newborns and toddlers, feeling their spirits wake up in new bodies— though their minds are still close to God and the clearheaded spirit of the north. East is the place to start again. Even the sun begins here each day as it travels its yellow path from east to west.

South is the busy place where young sprouts mature, eager to drink in as much nectar as they can, even while the winds change from wet to dry. The south brings the most potent rays of the sun, but also clarity and great swooping charges of energy. It's the direction of the first realization—both of self and of others. In the south, the needs of community begin to push selfish needs to the side. This is the prime of young adulthood and physical capability. At this age, we're not fully aware of our mortality. The lessons of life haven't yet inscribed themselves on our brow, yet we already begin to ripen into our fullness in this place. But as the noonday bell rings, we're usually too busy to notice the subtle shift from morning energy to afternoon languor and quiet. We're still at the peak, eating red ripe berries on a midsummer day. Yet the message of the south is responsibility. Though we may bask in summer heat and physical strength, we feel the days shorten and know that to fulfill our destiny, we must begin to share our power with others.

West is a full blossom on an autumn day, with heat in the afternoon and chill in the evening. It's the sunset, when colors, fruits and pumpkins grow shamelessly wild or huge and we trumpet our own full glory—sour notes and all. In the west we accept ourselves as we are, have been and are becoming. Yet, like a heavy-headed rose with browning petals, we express a new softness and humility. In the west, we work with others for the betterment of the world. Ego is not our lover in the western sky, as it often is in the east and south. By the time we reach the west, we've weathered rejection and have moved on into reflection and introspection. We shift out of the way of doing things that brought success in the south into unknown territory. The theme of the west is surrender and share. Dreams of the winter north sometimes flash like premonitions—or memories. We watch as the sun shrinks itself into a tiny speck and pulls with it our restless youth. Although winter is still a quarter of a lifetime away, its signs are everywhere. Leaves crackle on the ground; clouds grow thick and dark. Fruits hang from our trees bursting with the sweetest pulp, some of it yet untasted, when a sudden chill morning shrouds us in frost. In the west, we prepare for winter and cleanse ourselves of the wounds of youth, so that we may retire to a golf course and/or shaman time.

The Diagonals

Diagonal directions are symbols of transition. Northeast, southeast, southwest and northwest have the flavor of the directions in front of and behind them. Diagonals mark the betweentimes.

Northeast has the spirit-wisdom of the north but the will and desire of the east. It's the old soul preparing to reincarnate inside a new body.

Southeast brings the east's hunger for new experience and binds it to the desire for learning in the south. It is energy becoming consciously directed.

Southwest is Indian summer—the last grace of youthful, summer southern heat and the first signs of autumn's western maturity. In the southwest, we switch from gathering experience to sharing it with others.

Northwest brings us into the ripened wisdom of the elder, where we begin to fold back into darkness. We've almost completed a full revolution. Our time is almost up. Our spiral of understanding is almost complete.

The Movement Mandala

The Movement Mandala is a world of eights. It actually contains more than eight directions but it's easiest to grasp this concept if you just think in terms of eights.

Mandala as compass. Imagine yourself standing in the center of a compass etched on the floor. To get your bearings, find north—your front and center. (This doesn't have to be true north. It's more important that you get your bearings in *your* world.)

Now set your primary angles:

- In front of you is north.

- In back of you is south.

- To your right is east.

- To your left is west.

Now for your secondary angles:

- Your right front diagonal is northeast.

- Your right back diagonal is southeast.

- Your left front diagonal is northwest.

- Your left back diagonal is southwest.

If you are "directionally challenged," it might help to think of a map of the United States. The eastern seaboard represents the east, California the west, North Dakota the north and the tip of Texas the south. New England represents the northeast, the Carolinas southeast, Santa Fe the southwest and Seattle the northwest. However, the Movement Mandala is a *visual* map. You don't have to say or think "southwest" or "Santa Fe" every time. Just picture the space evenly divided into eight directions and know which direction you're aiming for.

Mandala as globe. Now imagine the compass as a 3-D orb like the planet Earth. Picture your vertical axis—the North and South Pole line. This axis should run up through the *center* point of your head and down through the *center* point between your feet. Where the North and South Poles meet is in your *center* of gravity—a few inches below your navel. This vertical axis is perhaps the most important line because it sets your alignment. You'll move off it all the time. But you should know how vertical looks and feels so you can always reestablish it.

Extend your arms directly out to the sides (east and west), parallel to the ground. It may help to think of this line as your equator or horizon. This horizontal line should form an exact 90-degree angle from the pole line.

Now lift both arms up, midway between the horizon and the North Pole.

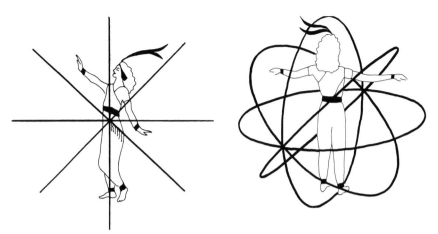

The Movement Mandala, Two Dimensions   The Movement Mandala, Three Dimensions

This will take your arms to the *upper* diagonals. To push this metaphor of body as globe, your hands will be on your body's equivalent of the Tropic of Cancer. Likewise, if you lower your arms midway down between the South Pole and the horizon, your arms will be on the *lower* diagonals—or your body's equivalent of the Tropic of Capricorn.

Try not to confuse north on the vertical axis (the "North Pole"), which is on your head, with north on the body compass, which is in front of you. You may find, as I do, that it's relatively easy to think "north, south, etc." for directions when you picture the mandala on the floor. But for this globe-shaped version, it's much simpler to divide the space as "up, down, horizontal, upper and lower diagonals." Eventually, these angles will "pattern" themselves on your body and you'll use them without thinking, which is good because thinking too logically doesn't mix well with movement—and can interrupt your spontaneity and pleasure.

The Movement Mandala doesn't quite end here. Bear with me if you will, as this next part may sound tricky—but it's not. You can marry the two- and three-dimensional aspects together with this simple exercise. Point your right arm to the northeast. Now lift that arm on an upper diagonal. Voila! You've got direction *and* dimension.

If you're having trouble visualizing any of this, don't worry. You'll understand the directions as you *use* them. You probably figured out the directions from looking at the illustrations, in a fraction of the time it took to read these words.

Simply start by becoming familiar with your angles and try to hit them precisely. Don't force a position, however, if it doesn't feel right for your body. As with a meditational mandala, the Movement Mandala is simply a guide or an ideal. But it's also a rebalancer. In other words, if you base exercises or choreography on the mandala, you may discover that you favor certain directions over others. For instance, most people are frontally and laterally oriented and seldom move backward or on the diagonals. As you become more conscious of these eight directions, you can overcome that imbalance by making sure you spend at least some time in all the directions. This can give you more balanced musculature and make your movements more aesthetically pleasing.

At first, some people feel a bit restricted by the mandala and don't want to be limited by these angles. They want to lift their arms to any point along the way. Of course, there's nothing wrong with that. But chances are good that if you follow these directions, your placement will be physiologically more sound, your lines will look better and the energy will run through you with fewer impediments.

If you've ever gone out dancing and found yourself on the dance floor next to someone who's had too many drinks and whose arms and legs thrash out like a drowning person's, you know that your first instinct is to move away as fast as you can. Random, scattered, chaotic moves put bodies at risk and jangle the spirit, whether you're watching or doing the moves. On the other hand (and this book is about the other hand), deliberate, devotionally placed moves bring deep satisfaction and joy.

The Movement Mandala, like a sand mandala, is impermanent. When you stop using it, it disappears. However, what it teaches gets stored in "muscle memory." When it starts to spill out by itself and structure all your movements, then it will be a permanent part of your movement life.

Moving in Balance

4 The Temple Dance Form

Thirteen Moves for Balance,
Strength and Grace

The arts of dancing and sculpture are too closely interdependent. . . . Our temple sculptures and icons are nothing but a vivid illustration of Indian classical dances in stone and metal. In this sense, every temple cave and shrine becomes essentially a sublime ensemble of mudras, poses, postures, stances and lineaments of movement and speed which are the essential components of dance. —B. R. KISHORE, *DANCES OF INDIA*

In the golden era of the Pallava and Chola kings [6th to 13th century A.D.], there arose in South India, great temples with towering gopurams, vast pillared halls and corridors adorned with sculptured gods of the Hindu pantheon and celestial dancers. In these magnificent shrines of the gods Shiva and Vishnu, holy ritual and dance were merged in a beautiful temple service—a sublime synthesis of art and religion.
—RAGINI DEVI, *DANCE DIALECTS OF INDIA*

This Temple Dance form is a series of movements inspired by statues of devadasis, which decorate the walls of temples throughout India, as well as postures from classical Indian dance. It borrows the notion of a "form," or choreographed series of moves from dance, tai chi and other martial arts. It borrows its essence from Hindu sacred dance, although this is *not* classical dance—only an *interpretation* of it. I created this form to make the spirit of the dance accessible to people with no dance training or desire to make the commitment to study the classical Indian styles—and to make it a workout.

This is a valid form of exercise. You can do this in a slow and lyrical fashion to emphasize placement, move quickly for a more cardiovascular experience or hold the postures for at least ten seconds each as if doing yoga. Any way you do it, it builds balance (by working the hip and torso stabilizers), creates strength in the lower body and torso, improves alignment and enhances all-over grace. I use it as warm-up for a yoga class or cool-down at the end of a dance class. I also use it as my "dancer's tai chi form" to awaken my Shakti energy in the mornings before I write. This versatile series of movements is simple enough for beginners but has enough spirit and sensibility of the original temple dances to satisfy more experienced movers.

There are thirteen movements, although the first is really just a prayer, so there are twelve main moves. Thirteen is an appropriate number for a woman's form, however, because there are thirteen full moons—and therefore, usually thirteen menstrual cycles—every year. Thirteen is considered an unlucky number *because* of its ties to nature and women and therefore has pagan connections. However, as more women embrace feminine spiritual traditions, thirteen is regaining respect—and it "just happens" to work well here.

Doing the form increases the flow of blood, oxygen and "chi" (life energy) in a very soothing, balanced way, just as tai chi and chi kung do. I can't prove this but I feel it.

The form will definitely work your mind—especially at first—and maybe too much. In the initial learning stage, you'll be asked to be aware of your posture, your placement within the Movement Mandala, the hand positions (mudras) and the story that each movement tells. Try not to get overwhelmed by memorizing everything at once or doing each movement perfectly. Focus first on the legs and torso, then add the arms and hands. Finally add the story and the feeling behind each move. After a while, the mechanics should become more automatic. If you forget a move or mudra, don't worry. This is not so much an exercise in choreography and sequence as it is a devotional dance. Feel free to add your own movements or self-expression, change the positions to better suit your body or simply borrow one or two moves to use elsewhere. Keep in mind that the most beautiful aspect of this form is that it lets you enter the *spirit* of the temple dancer.

The Six Postures

The Vertical Posture

The lyrical curve of the body is very unique to classical Indian dance. It may take you a while to get used to holding the curved positions. But they're also very natural and, unless you have a severe hip injury, should feel good to do and will loosen up your hips. (If you do have hip problems, ease your way into the curved positions and don't curve so far that it causes pain.) The following six basic postures provide a foundation for all the movements you'll do in the form.

The vertical posture. This is your starting, ending and return-to-neutral position—a posture of serenity and devotion. Let the vertical axis run from the

Hips off the Vertical

Upper Body off the Vertical

The Triple Bend

The Wide Stance

The Knee Sit

crown of your head, down your tailbone and between the heels. With heels touching, turn out the toes to 10 and 2 o'clock. Soften your knees. Lift your chest slightly. Relax and pull back your shoulders. Hands are in the mudra "prayer hands" (palms touching in front of chest, as in the Opening Prayer).

Hips off the vertical. Your weight is mostly on one leg as you thrust out one hip to the side into an elegant, stately posture. The curve can be as big or as subtle as you want. The movements Honor the Mother, Honor the Audience, Bending Like a Branch of a Tree (move B) and Saraswati all use hips off the vertical line.

Upper body off the vertical. Here the hips stay centered as the upper body pulls off the vertical. Your weight can be on one leg or two, as in the movements Pick a Flower off a Tree and Smell It, Bliss and Reverence (move A), Dancing with Bells and Cymbals (move B) and Radha.

The triple bend. This is the most unique posture—and what makes Indian dance look so enchanting. One hip pulls in one direction, the shoulders in the other—as in the movements Prayer to Ganesh, Bending Like a Branch of a Tree (move A) and Krishna—and the top of the head curves toward the extended hip. In addition, one arm typically crosses the midline of the body. (If you can't get the head posture, don't worry. Focus more on the opposition between shoulder and hip.)

The wide stance. This is a wide, deep, heroic stance. Your weight is evenly distributed between both legs although you can later shift your weight onto one leg. Use ballet's second-position grand plié here. (Your legs should be set about two to three times wider than your hips, with your feet turned to 10 and 2 o'clock. Keep your heels down.) You'll use this in the movement Divine Enchantress and to prepare for the Shiva move.

The knee sit. This isn't really a classical posture but a very useful one that lets you crouch down and incline your torso forward without putting any strain on your lower back or knees. Stand with one leg in front of the other and the back heel up, both knees slightly bent. Both feet can remain slightly turned out. As you bend your knees, touch the front of one knee to the back of the other, so they fit inside each other, like nesting plates. This supports your thighs, hips and back so you can "sit" down safely and comfortably, as you will do in Offering and Benediction (move B), Bliss and Reverence (move B) and Krishna.

General Points

Oppositions. When you pull in one direction, pull another part of your body in the opposite direction. This creates dynamic tension, which creates balance. Your center and anchor of stability will always be in the hip/navel area.

Directions. Use the Movement Mandala to be clear about the directions you're facing and moving in. Use your upper and lower diagonals to create pleasing lines.

Differentiate between lines and curves. Be aware if the move is round or straight, especially when you're holding a posture.

Hold each posture for at least a second before flowing into the next position.

Mudras. The beautiful hand gestures of Indian dance represent both art and science. The artful side of mudra making is apparent. But the science behind it is based on an amazingly refined, ancient understanding of how the architecture of movement affects internal energy. In other words, various hand positions supposedly access different degrees of electrical energy (also called *prana* or *kundalini*). Yoginis, therefore, not only used their hands to dazzle observers with their beauty and storytelling ability, they also controlled the flow of subtle energy—and could supposedly redirect that energy and share it with others. I must admit, using mudras to access and redirect kundalini is beyond my comprehension. I use mudras for their beauty, their devotional content, to bring awareness to the small muscles in the hands and because they seem to "complete" each movement. If *you* find that your mudras access electrical energy—great! Tell me about it! I'd love to know. (Incidentally, there are more than one hundred mudras. In this form, we use only a few.)

Story. Many types of dance tell stories, act out daily activities or reveal something of the human heart. But Indian classical dances do these things perhaps more intricately and elegantly than all other styles. To fully appreciate Indian classical dance, even from the audience, you need a basic understanding of what some of the gestures mean so you can follow the story. It's not my intention here to supply you with all that information, and you don't need any previous knowledge of these styles or the Hindu myths in order to do this form. The story line is intentionally simple (each move is a story unto itself) and is there simply to give each movement purpose and emotion, so that *you* can enhance your expression. Indirectly, this will also make you a better performer, if that's important to you. If the stories or emotions I suggest don't ring true to you, feel free to supply your own!

Learn the form slowly. Learn only one or two moves a day. If you try to learn too many moves at once, they won't imprint as effectively on your muscle memory. Many moves consist of two to three motions—so each offers much to "chew on." At this pace it should take one to three weeks to learn the whole form. When you're learning a new move, dissect it, play with it, make it your own. Don't worry about "doing it right." It's more important to let it *feel* right. After you've imprinted a new move on your body, start the whole form from the top and add the new move on the end. (Hint: These were designed in sequence to make it flow. However, if you put something out of order, most of the time it'll fit almost anywhere).

Repetitions. I've given you numbers of repetitions for each move but these are only guidelines. Do each move two, four or eight times—in some multiple of two. (I usually do each move a total of four times—twice on each side.) Even numbers give your body a balanced workout and let you sync your moves to music, if you choose to use it. (However, if you use music, don't be bullied by a particular tempo. Go off the rhythm as you please. Use a slow tempo—about 60 to 120 beats per minute—or use no rhythm. You'll notice that some moves are faster than others so don't try to make them all fit into the same counts.)

Each move should take at least two seconds for the simpler motions, four to eight seconds for the more complex ones. Slower is harder because you *have* to call on your balance and muscle, not momentum. It's also harder because most of us are used to moving to fast tempos either in aerobics class or in life and feel that going slow holds us back. In fact, slow tempos can quickly reveal where you need extra work on balance and strength. Completing the whole form takes approximately ten to fifteen minutes.

Breathe normally. Exhales fit best with long stretches.

Memory. The form has three separate sections (Blessings, Lyrical Dancers and Gods and Goddesses) and each has four moves. It's easier to remember three sections of four movements than twelve separate motions.

All moves begin with the right side first so you never have to think about it.

Return to the vertical posture after completing a move (heels touching, prayer hands) before doing that move on the other side or moving on to the next motion. This puts you back in "neutral."

The Temple Dance Form

1. Opening Prayer

Stand in the vertical posture, facing north, heels touching, toes turned out, palms of the hands together. Lift your hands overhead and then lower them into two other positions—from overhead to face, then to chest. Let your eyes and head follow your hands. When your hands are:

Over your head, acknowledge the Spirit.

In front of your face, honor your human teachers and guides.

At your chest, bow to your peers.

Start facing north; begin with hands overhead and lower them through the two other positions. Turn east and repeat the gesture there, and so on to the four main directions on the Movement Mandala.

Mudra This mudra is called "prayer hands," or salutation. Palms are touching; fingers are closed and straight, thumbs are pulled in. This basic mudra shows devotion to deities and humans.

Story As you face each direction, think or recite something like this:

"As we face north, we pray to our ancestors, to the wisdom of our elders, to winter sleep and the place where souls originate and return."

"As we face east, we pray to the spirit of reborn souls, spring's renewal and our own new beginnings."

"As we face south, we pray to the potent rays of summer sun, to the strength of our own young adulthood and to becoming responsible to our power."

"As we face west, we pray to the ripeness and maturity of our soul's passage, to the autumn harvest of our experience, and to sharing our wisdom with others."

Transition to each direction Take a quarter turn to the right.

Suggested reps 1 round of 4 reps.

Transition to the next move Face north in your vertical posture, with heels touching and the mudra "prayer hands" in front of the chest.

2. Offering and Benediction

Do moves A and B in succession before repeating A and B again.

Inspiration	The opening offering prayer (called a *pranam*) that begins classical Indian dances.
Move A: The Offering	Step forward (north) onto right foot, keeping right knee bent (left heel stays up to prepare for the knee sit in move B). Both feet are slightly turned out. Look up as you lift arms up the vertical axis.
Mudra	Hands are cupped together, forming a "double lotus blossom," fingers wide like a bowl.
Story	Present a lotus to the spirits of heaven as a gift of devotion from your heart.

Move B: **The Benediction**	As you lower your arms, open your chest to the ceiling and receive the blessing. Touch knees together for the knee sit. This will support your back as you incline your torso forward. Take the spine parallel to the floor (the horizontal line) or, if that's too hard on your back, lower the spine to the upper diagonal. Keep arms behind the back, on the same line as the spine. After holding this position, bring the hands back to prayer hands and bring the spine up the vertical line, initiating the move from the hips. (Don't round the back up. It's easier on your back to come up straight, especially if your weight is back in your hips.)
Mudra	Touch the thumb to the middle finger as you raise your arms behind you. Lift the other fingers. This mudra, a variation of one called "lion's face," also symbolizes fragrance, pearls, salvation.
Story	Receive the grace of the gods. Feel the warm love pouring down on you from heaven.
Transition to the other side	Switch feet so the left foot's in front. Start again and repeat moves A and B.
Works	Abdominal and back stabilizers, buttocks, thighs.
Stretches	Chest, shoulders, abdominals, hamstrings and buttocks.
Be sure you	Don't round the back as you lean the torso forward in the knee sit. Keep abdominals pulled in and the chest lifted.
Suggested reps	4.
Transition to the next move	Return to vertical posture.

Inspiration	Statue of devadasi in Chidambaram temple.
Move	Put your right hand on your right hip. Extend the left arm out to the west. Your stance should be about as wide as your hips. Keep your knees slightly bent. Circle the right hip 8 times counterclockwise. If you could "draw" that circle with your hips, you'd leave a mark on the wall in front of you (not on the floor).
Mudra	The hand on the extended arm is in "creeper pose"—the arm resembles a creeping vine. The extended elbow is bent, the hand relaxed, the wrist slightly curved. The other hand rests on the hip or thigh.
Story	With the gentle sway of your hips, honor Mother Earth, who pours her fruitfulness through your own hips. Honor your own feminine spirit as well and the Shakti energy that runs through you, for you are a daughter of the Earth.
Transition to the other side	Circle the other hip 8 times clockwise, switch arms.
Works	Abdominal and hip muscles.

Stretches	Abdominal and hip muscles. (The circular motion allows these muscles to work and stretch in one motion.)
Be sure you	Aim for full circles. This move warms up the hips for the other moves that follow.
Suggested reps	8 in each direction.
Transition to the next move	Return to vertical posture. Then bend your left knee.

4. Honor the Audience

Inspiration	Line drawing of devadasi performing at Puri temple in Jagannath, twelfth century A.D.
Move	Step the right leg out to the northeast. Keep the right foot flexed and right knee bent. Sink down into your left supporting leg and sit your left hip to the west. Imagine that you're holding a basket in your left arm. With your right hand gracefully take a flower out of the basket and offer it to those who respectfully observe. This should incline your torso slightly forward on an upper diagonal.

Keep your back straight. Repeat on the other side (stepping out with left foot and gesturing with your left hand).

Mudra	The forefinger and middle finger touch the thumb. The pinkie is straight up, while the ring finger lifts halfway up. This mudra, called "swan face," symbolizes an offering, affection, purity, also instruction in ritual.
Story	Honor anyone who is present with you today, whether in physical form or in spirit, and give from your heart. Look lovingly into the eyes of those who receive the flowers.
Transition to the other side	To switch sides, simply step onto your other foot and shift your weight into that other hip.
Works	Buttocks, thighs, lower back and abdominals.
Stretches	Hamstrings, buttocks, lower back.
Be sure you	Keep your back straight (a little arch in the lower back is okay, but don't round it). Keep your extended leg slightly bent.
Suggested reps	2 to 4 each side.
Transition to the next move	Return to vertical posture, facing north.

5. Prayer to Ganesh

Prayer to Ganesh

Inspiration	Many Odissi dances begin with a prayer to Ganesh to remove any obstacles in the way of expressing devotion. Ganesh is the good-natured, elephant-headed son of Shiva and Shakti (see move #12), who clears away difficulties and creates a spiritual path for a believer. Ganesh is reportedly also capable of thinking like a human and so he understands the nature of our requests. Worship of Ganesh is thought to be immediate; as you think of him, you contact him (his goodness travels at cyber speed).

Move With your torso facing north, step to the east. Sink down into the right leg and jut the hip to the east. Pull the left foot in close to the right and raise the heel. This is the triple bend posture. *Pull shoulders to the west*. Lift the right arm to the upper diagonal (your elbow is bent). Take the left arm across the body, on the horizontal line. To add the head position, look out over your left elbow (to the northwest) and drop your head into your raised right arm. (Your head will be tilted on an upper diagonal.)

Mudra Fingers are together, palms are flat and facing out and to the ceiling. This mudra, called "banner hands," shows your devotion to both deities and humans. The hands are in the same position as prayer hands but instead of touching palms together, expose them to your audience so they see your openness.

Story Typically one prays to Ganesh with these thoughts: "Please remove any difficulties or obstructions in my life right now which are preventing me from experiencing divine love."

Transition to the other side	Step out to the west with your left foot, sink weight into that hip and repeat. Both arms and hips follow a semicircular path down and up to the other side.
Works	Hip and torso stabilizers, thighs.
Stretches	Outer hip and back of shoulders.
Be sure you	Sink your weight down into your leg and foot before setting the hip out to the side.
Suggested reps	8 total, 4 each side.
Transition to the next move	Return to vertical posture.

PART 2. LYRICAL DANCERS

6. *Pick a Flower off a Tree and Smell It*

	Do moves A and B one after the other, 2 to 4 times on the same side, then switch sides and repeat.
Inspiration	The Hindu love of nature as an expression of the divine.
Move A: Pick a Flower off a Tree	Step the right foot back to the southeast corner. Your right arm traces an arc over your head. Look back at your right hand as you imagine picking a beautiful magnolia blossom. Your left hand stays in front of your heart. Left foot steps behind the right to the southeast. You'll need your balance here because your torso pulls to the southeast corner (the upper body moves off the vertical line).
Mudra	The middle and ring fingers touch the thumb while the pinkie and forefinger remain lifted and straight. This mudra, "lion's face," often represents fragrance. It's also used as a salutation when placed near the heart.

Story   Take hold of a beautiful magnolia blossom. Feel the soft petals in your hand. Pick it and draw it toward you.

Move B: Smell It	Step to the northwest corner, bringing both feet together. Retrace the arc over your head, so it comes in front of your face. Bend the knees, put your weight on both feet and incline the torso slightly forward on an upper diagonal, keeping the back neutral (with a slight arch in your lower back). Cross the wrists, so the hands are on either side of your face.
Mudra	Keep the hands in lion's face, as above.
Story	Smell the sweet blossoms. Take a moment to inhale the perfume.
Transition to the other side	After repeating at least twice on one side, return to the vertical posture. Step back to the southwest corner to repeat on the other side.
Works	Hip and torso stabilizers, shoulders.
Stretches	Chest.
Be sure you	Step securely onto your supporting leg for move A. Remember to sink your weight down. This way you can fully reach your arm up and back. For move B, keep your lower back slightly arched and chest lifted. Don't round the back. Keep the weight on both feet.

Suggested reps	2 to 4 in one direction, 2 to 4 in the other.
Transition to the next step	Return to vertical posture.

7. *Bliss and Reverence*

Do moves A and B one after the other, at least twice on the same side, then switch sides and repeat.

Inspiration	Statues in Konarak temple, thirteenth century A.D.
Move A: Bliss	Cross your right leg over your left, keeping the left heel up. (Right toes face north, left toes face northwest.) Face the northwest corner. Both knees remain slightly bent to prepare for the knee sit in move B. Lift your left arm up over your head, so the palm of your hand is in line with the center of your head.

Stretch your whole left side, tipping the chest up to the sky. Your right hand rests on your hip.

Mudra   The upturned palm is flat and facing the sky to honor the gods. Fingers and thumbs are closed. Again, you're using the "banner hands" mudra. In this posture it represents victory, divine assurance and grace. It's a way of saying, "I am here."

Story   Let the bliss flow through you as you offer your beauty and grace as a gift to the gods.

Move B: Reverence   Still facing the northwest corner, bend your back knee so it touches the back of your right knee and lower into the knee sit. Sit your *hips back* and incline your *torso forward* on an upper diagonal. Arms move to the horizontal plane. Right arm is extended. Left hand rests near the heart. Look out over your extended arm.

Mudra   Again, with banner hands, place one hand by your heart and look out over your extended arm. The open palm of the straight arm offers a benediction to anyone who observes, and it demonstrates your own divine self-assurance.

Story	Feel grateful for the bliss that runs through you. Acknowledge how much devotion adds to your life and, in turn, with the power you feel, bless others.
Transition to the other side	Repeat 2 to 4 times with right foot front then return to the vertical posture. Cross the left foot over the right and face the northeast as you repeat on the other side.
Works	Move A works the upper back and one shoulder. Move B works the buttocks, thighs, shoulders and torso stabilizers.
Stretches	Move A stretches your sides. Move B stretches your buttocks and chest.
Be sure you	Keep knees close enough so they can touch for the knee sit. As the knees touch, you can sit back in your hips as if in a "chair" and maintain lower back support. Remember to keep your back straight as you incline forward.
Suggested reps	2 to 4 with right foot in front, 2 to 4 with left foot in front.
Transition to the next step	Return to vertical posture.

8. Bending Like a Branch of a Tree

Do moves A and B one after the other, then switch sides and repeat.

**Bending Like a Branch
(one way)**

Inspiration Statues from Lingaraj temple, eighth century A.D.

**Move A
(Bending One Way)** Cross your right foot over your left. Lift the left heel. Both feet are slightly turned out and both knees are bent. Lace your fingers together, lift the arms overhead (vertical) and turn the palms up. Lower the arms to the right upper diagonal and lift the right hip. (Bring elbow and hip toward each other.) This stretches the entire left side of your body.

Mudra This mudra, called "crab" in this position (with arms overhead and palms up), symbolizes bending a tree branch, yawning, stretching.

Story Flexibility of body and spirit is the dancer's greatest asset. Plant your feet like the roots of a tree but keep your limbs and your mind flexible to the changes around you.

Move B (Bending the Other Way) Hold the posture from move A (keep hips and arms to the right) as you extend the left leg to the west. Then lower arms, undo fingers and lean torso to the west (torso ends up on an upper diagonal). Right arm is on the upper diagonal (opposite the torso). Left arm is on the lower diagonal. Look down at the fingers on the lower hand.

Mudra The "full-blown lotus" is one of the most beautiful mudras. Separate the fingers by starting with the little finger. This mudra stands for beauty, joy, radiance, and the sun.

Story As the trunk of your torso bends from one side to the other, allow the bend to enhance, not break, your line. With the grounding power of a loving spirit, conditions don't have to break you. They can make you more beautiful.

Transition to the other side Cross the left foot over the right. Interlace the fingers and lift arms and hip to the left. Repeat moves A and B on this side. You'll be alternating sides.

Works Hip and torso stabilizers.

Stretches	The entire sides of the body.
Be sure you	Keep your hip jutted to one side while you extend your leg and lower your torso to the other. This is what gives the movement drama and dynamic tension.
Suggested reps	2 to 4 on each side.
Transition to the next step	Return to vertical position.

9. Dancing with Bells and Cymbals

Do moves A and B one after the other, 2 to 4 times on the same side, then switch sides and repeat.

Dancing with Bells

Inspiration	Temple statues, location and date uncertain.
Move A: Dancing with Bells	Lift the right leg to the northwest corner. Raise the right arm overhead so hand aligns with vertical. (Same arm and leg are lifted.) The palm of the right hand is aligned over the head, on the vertical.

Mudra	Palms are flat, fingers together but thumb open in this "half-moon" position. Both palms face out. This mudra symbolizes the moon and its inward qualities (meditation, consecration).
Story	Raise the leg as if you had bells on your ankles (you can even shake your ankle a little, if you want). The bells make the sounds of the gods. Take a moment to "hear" that sound.

Dancing with Cymbals

Move B: Dancing with Cymbals	Bring your right foot down next to your left foot. Then step the left foot back to the southeast corner (be sure to keep your right knee bent as you do this). Left leg can straighten. Stretch your torso and tilt the head slightly back.
Mudra	Hold your hands by your left ear, palms touching (in prayer hands), as if you were playing cymbals in your ear. Clap if you want to.
Story	The cymbals create the sound of ecstasy. Feel the ecstasy. Take it in.
Transition to the other side	After 2 to 4 repetitions on one side, return to neutral and repeat on the other side. (Lift the left leg and arm. Step back with the right.)

Works	Supporting legs and torso stabilizers.
Stretches	Both sides of the torso.
Be sure you	Slightly bend your supporting knee.
Suggested reps	4 pairs, 2 each side.
Transition to the next step	Return to vertical posture.

PART 3. GODS AND GODDESSES

10. Krishna and Radha

Do 2 to 4 Krishna moves, followed by 2 to 4 Radha moves.

Krishna is the beloved, flute-playing herder of cows. He's playful and flirtatious and his melodies lure the milkmaids from their homes to dance with him in the moonlight. He was considered an incarnation of Vishnu, the god of preservation, the one who maintains all of life. The love between Krishna and

the beautiful Radha is the theme of countless paintings and poems (the *Gita Govinda* is the most famous). Krishna and Radha seem to embody the romantic side of human love, with all its heights and foibles. He teases, she waits; he chases after her, she runs away and then looks for him; he hides and finally throws a loving arm around her.

Inspiration The passion of Krishna and Radha also symbolizes devotion to God.

Move A: Krishna Plays His Flute Step out to the east with the right foot. Cross the left foot behind (to the southeast) and lower into a partial knee sit. Arms travel in a semicircular path, from left to right, tracing the lower half of a circle. Head can turn away from the flute. Eyes are playful.

Mudra Thumbs touch middle and forefingers in the "lion's face" mudra. Position the hands to mimic playing a flute. On the hand closest to the face, point the fingers toward you. On the hand farthest from the face, turn the fingers out.

Story In a coy, flirtatious mood, play a seductive melody on your flute to capture the attention of the young Radha.

Transition to the other side Simply step out with left foot and back with the right. Bring arms in a low semicircle to the left. Repeat this step 2 to 4 times before switching to move B.

Move B: Radha Hides Behind Her Veil	Step the right foot to the east and bring the left foot next to it. The knees touch and close in a demure position. The arms move in a figure 8 in front of the face (passing between the upper and lower diagonals). The expression is shy but coy.
Mudra	Extend the forefinger and middle finger (Radha holds her veil with these two fingers). Bend the thumb to hold down the ring finger and pinkie. This mudra, called "scissor mouth," indicates opposites, differences, also (when fingers are farther apart) the separation of a husband and wife. Allow the wrists to turn as you flutter the veil in front of your face.
Story	Hide and then reveal yourself with the veil. Feel both your shyness and your willingness to be seen.
Works	Thighs, buttocks, hip and torso stabilizers and shoulders.
Stretches	Buttocks, lower back and shoulders.
Be sure you	Keep your back straight as you incline your chest for the knee sit.
Suggested reps	2 to 4 Krishnas, followed by 2 to 4 Radhas.
Transition to the next move	Open legs into the wide stance (ballet's second-position plié). This puts feet at least twice as wide apart as the hips. Turn your feet out slightly (to 10 and 2 o'clock).

11. Divine Enchantress

Inspiration	Mohini Attam, a distinct south Indian dance form. In Hindu mythology, Lord Vishnu (the "preserver of life," the "Lord of the Universe"), disguised himself as a beautiful woman named Mohini in order to deceive the invading Titans. His enchanting dance seduced and defeated the enemy. Like the Krishna and Radha story, classical Indian dancers have used this story in many dance dramas. Yet in southern India, this story evolved as its own distinct style with a wide stance, a torso that swings from side to side and large, erotic eyes. In some versions of the dance, dancers seduced the enemy by playing with a real or imaginary ball—here we're seducing with flowers. For many years, the dance of the Mohini wasn't danced because of the association between temple dancing, seduction and prostitution. But now, as attitudes change again, the dance is being revived.

Move	Adopt the wide stance, with legs about 2½ times wider apart than hips, feet turned to 10 and 2 o'clock. Bend your knees. Rotate the torso 4 times in one direction and 4 in the other. Let your circle move more to the front than the back (to protect your lower back). As your trunk reaches back, however, use abdominal strength to stabilize and protect your torso. This is a safe, strengthening move as long as you control the width of your rotation.
Mudra	This mudra, called "flower basket," is an offering. Hands cup together, palms up, fingers together as if holding a bouquet, a ball or cupping water.
Story	Offer your sweet, playful, fragrant bounty. Let your rotating torso and expression create a hypnotic mood.
Transition to the other side	After 2 or 4 torso rotations in one direction, reverse.
Works	Lower back, abdominals, legs (in isometric contraction) and some chest and shoulders.
Stretches	Lower back and abdominals.

Be sure you	Keep elbows comfortably close to your body. The farther you extend your arms from your torso, the harder it is on your back.
Suggested reps	2 to 4 clockwise, 2 to 4 counterclockwise.
Transition to the next step	Stay in this wide stance and open the arms to east and west, palms up.

12. Shiva and Shakti

Do move A with Shiva Arms #1, then add Shiva Arms #2. Finish with move B and return to the wide stance before switching sides.

Shiva

Inspiration	The famous posture of Shiva. Shiva is the dancer at the center of the universe, dancing in his mandala of fire, the energy of pure consciousness. This fire protects him as he undergoes the dance of transformation (because transformation can be painful). Shakti, the feminine force that gives the spark of life to all

things, propels him. Shiva, the god of both creation and destruction, also represents many more apparent opposites: stillness and motion, matter and spirit, masculine and feminine, sexuality and asceticism. Shiva's four-armed posture is full of meaning.

- His upper right hand holds a drum (a damaru), which beats the primal rhythm of creation.

- His lower right hand is lifted in the "half-moon" mudra, as a sign of blessing, a way of saying, "have no fear."

- In his upper left hand, he holds fire, the symbol of cleansing destruction.

- His lower left hand crosses the body with the palm facing down. It's an obscuring posture, one that hides his grace—a symbol for hiding the truth (or keeping the truth hidden, in the esoteric tradition of revealing it only to those who can handle it). The left hand also points down to a small demon, which signifies ignorance, underfoot. Shiva, very gracefully and compassionately, stomps on his body.

- Shiva's left leg is lifted in a posture that shows his grace.

Move A:
Shiva Arms #1

From the wide-stanced Divine Enchantress pose you've just done, shift all your weight onto your right leg (so you can raise the left). Keep arms open on a horizontal line, palms up as you lift your left leg to the northeast corner.

Mudra

Hands maintain the half-moon position throughout—the gesture of Shiva, indicating hope and fearlessness. Flatten the palms, keep fingers together and open the thumbs.

Story

Honor the great Shiva, lover of Shakti, and the union of the masculine and feminine, creation, destruction, the full cycle of dark, light, death and rebirth. Your expression should be powerful and wise.

Move A:
Shiva Arms #2

Maintain that leg position as you change arms. Cross the left arm over your body (to the northeast corner) and point the left fingers down. Bend the right elbow so it's higher than or in line with your wrist (arms stay horizontal). Raise the right palm so it faces north.

Mudra and story

Same as above.

Move B: Shakti	Raise your right arm on the upper diagonal. Left arm stays across the body and horizontal. The left leg either extends out to the west on a lower diagonal (foot touching the floor) or you can raise the foot and bend the knee so the bottom part of the leg is horizontal to the floor.
Mudra	Soften the fingers into a beautiful, lyrical pose. This is not a specific mudra— simply an erotically feminine, irresistibly gorgeous pair of hands.
Story	Honor and express the feminine Shakti energy, which sustains Shiva and every living thing. Be humble, delicate, loving, affectionate. Keep your expression soft yet remain aware of your own divinity.
Transition to the other side	Return to the wide stance (as in the Divine Enchantress), shift weight to the left leg and repeat Shiva and Shakti on that side.
Works	Thigh of supporting leg, shoulders, hip and torso stabilizers.
Stretches	Buttocks (in Shiva posture) and the whole side of the body (in Shakti posture).

Be sure you	Shift your weight onto your supporting leg *before* you lift the other. Remember: shift, then lift.
Suggested reps	4 total, 2 each side.
Transition to the next step	After your last Shakti pose, return to vertical posture.

13. Brahma and Saraswati

Do moves A and B in succession before switching sides.

Brahma

Brahma is God, the supreme creator, the male force of creative energy (different from Shiva, who embodies creation and destruction). His creations include air, fire, water, earth, vegetation, food and humanity. Saraswati is his female counterpart, the mother of creativity, especially in the arts and sciences. She is always smiling and her beauty is "more powerful than the light of ten million moons."

Inspiration	Yoga's Tree pose, and statues at Konarak temple, thirteenth century A.D.
Move A: Brahma	Lift your right leg and rest the foot on your left thigh (a yoga Tree pose). You can simultaneously lift your right arm up the vertical line. (The same arm and leg lift.) The left arm stays down on the vertical. Imagine you're pulling a string between both fingers. Pull up through the head and down through the feet and tailbone to maintain balance.
Mudra	Touch your thumb to your middle and ring finger, once again in the "lion's face" mudra. Keep your other fingers raised. Imagine you're holding the sacred thread of all creation.
Story	In this posture, realign with the masculine, linear and vertical forces of creation. Keep your expression steady, all-knowing and calm. Brahma's posture signifies logic and power.

Move B: Saraswati	Sink your weight down into your supporting leg and then sit the left hip farther to the left (west). The upper parts of the arms form a horizontal line. But the forearms align on upper and lower diagonals. Look toward the lower hand.

Mudra	Maintain the same "lion's face" mudra as above.
Story	As goddess of education and the arts, Saraswati has a radiance "as white as the moon" and is beautifully adorned in jeweled stones and pearls. Let your expression be soft, wise and radiant. Feel abundantly jeweled, talented and beautiful.
Transition to the other side	Lift the left leg and arm and repeat moves A and B on the other side.
Works	Thighs, hip and torso stabilizers.
Stretches	Outer hip.
Be sure you	Sink down into your leg before shifting your weight out into your hip. Also, realign your body to vertical before switching sides.
Suggested reps	4 total (2 each side).
Transition to finish	Return to vertical posture. Repeat the Opening Prayer gesture at least once (hands above head, in front of face, in front of chest) as closure and thanks.

Quick Recap

Opening Prayer

Part 1. Blessings

Offering and Benediction

Honor the Mother

Honor the Audience

Prayer to Ganesh

Part 2. Lyrical Dancers

Pick a Flower off a Tree and Smell It

Bliss and Reverence

Bending Like a Branch of a Tree

Dancing with Bells and Cymbals

Part 3. Gods and Goddesses

Krishna and Radha

Divine Enchantress

Shiva and Shakti

Brahma and Saraswati

This entire Temple Dance form is featured in the last segment of *The WomanPower Workout* video (see page 222), and it is easier to follow from the video than this book. However, all the history, stories and explanations of mudras are here. For a complete understanding of this form, I recommend studying both.

Although the Temple Dance form will enhance your flexibility and lower-body strength, it's not meant as a prescription for "total fitness." For that, of course, you will need to put cardiovascular exercise in your life three to five days a week (dance, walk fast, swim, bike, etc.), and add strength training and flexibility—both of which are covered next. The Temple Dance form, however, is powerful enough to "seduce" you into an altered state. But you can also be seduced into similar states while doing yoga, dancing and even less enticing things like strength training. Using images, story and emotion can make all your fitness activities more interesting, fun and ecstatic.

5   You Can Be a Muscle Yogini

What is a "Muscle Yogini"? It's a woman who uses her body, imagination and emotions together to create magical, transcendental and even ecstatic exercise experiences. Anyone can be a Muscle Yogini. You don't have to be strong, "buffed" or "ripped." All you need is sensitivity to your body, feelings and spirit and a willingness to fall into a "workout trance." You must also refuse to put up with exercise you hate or situations in which you're just "going through the motions." Sometimes this means simply changing your thinking so that you are present every time you train and honor your body's changes and feedback. You need to let yourself fall in love with what you're doing—or at least yourself while you're doing it.

To initiate yourself into the way of the Muscle Yogini, you must work your muscles *slowly* and with good form! Slow motion keeps your muscles in a more constant state of contraction—which makes the experience more humbling and intense—but it works because it helps you maintain good form. When you move too fast, momentum takes over. You lose alignment and end up working a different set of muscles from the ones you *think* you're working—and thus you get minimal results and can hurt yourself. As you progress on this path, you'll know that whenever your form falls apart during an exercise, you should either finish the set with lighter resistance or stop.

I became a Muscle Yogini in my thirties, when I began to trust my body's feedback and pursued my *own* approach to training instead of following the often manic advice of muscle magazines and bodybuilders. Now, more than thirteen years later, I'm not as "ripped" or "buffed" as I was during my obsessive years (when I competed in a few amateur bodybuilding competitions). But my strength is about 85 percent of what it was at my peak. I also don't feel the need to lift as much or as often as I used to. I'm very clear that I continue to cultivate my strength to enjoy my own company, to function better in life and to support my passion—dance! I've also changed my eating habits since I wrote my first book and now maintain a mostly vegetarian diet rich in soy (outlined in chapter 8). I feel strong, lean, balanced and healthy.

Still, I'm aware that *packaging* strength to other women in an appealing way is the most challenging part of my job. So when I train others and teach classes, I do for others what I do alone—I orchestrate the exercises into an elegant dance. I may use music, my voice, images, breathing, chanting, creative moaning and well-placed pockets of silence to invoke a workout trance. Not everyone immediately falls under the seductive spell of these "muscle meditations." But eventually everyone's form becomes strong, everyone's tolerance increases and the muscles, by default, get stronger and learn to *crave* the sensation of hard work (even when the mind still disagrees). You'll know *you've* become a Muscle Yogini when you maintain your grace in the discomfort, can put your mind completely *into* what you're doing or send it elsewhere at will but still maintain good form. Falling in love with muscle work can only serve your life, particularly as you get older and witness the huge gap between those who maintain their strength and those who do not. Which camp do *you* want to be in? To maintain strength throughout a lifetime, you only need to dance with discomfort for a few passing moments each week. But the goodness that you build in yourself along the way stays forever.

Selling Muscle

After all these years, I find myself still answering that same old question, "But what if I get big muscles?" My standard answer to this is: That's like worrying about becoming too happy, enlightened or rich. Let's not get stuck here, okay? Once again, for the record, women's muscles don't necessarily get *bigger* as they get stronger—not even after decades of focused training. They can get harder, leaner and shapelier and help you shed fat (because having more lean muscle speeds up your metabolism). But only approximately 1 in 100,000 women has the genetic "winning combination" to "get big." Here's what you'd need to grow big, "manly" muscles:

- Short limbs (or, more precisely, short "levers"). Shorter arms, legs and torso give you a "leverage advantage" over a person with long limbs and consequently make it easier for you to lift weight and get stronger. Short limbs also take less time to fill with strong muscle. Thus, "short-levered" lifters also *look* stronger than other people do.

- Long "muscle bellies" with short connective tissue (a very rare combo; most people have average-size limbs, short muscle bellies and long connective tissue).

- More than the average amount of testosterone for women (a genetic matter, which is not within your control, unless you do what some female bodybuilders do and inject it—which I emphatically advise against).

In addition, you'd need to train hard and intelligently with:

- Intense, short, moderate to heavy workouts (about forty-five minutes of high intensity training two days a week). (For more on how often to train, see "In Praise of Shorter, Less Frequent Workouts" on page 75.)

- An obsessive desire to keep track of every gram of carbohydrates, protein and fat that you eat (which makes you a real bore to dine out with).

- Additional time for aerobics (and you can easily overtrain with all of this) and yoga-type stretches to refresh tired muscles. But that still doesn't leave you enough time to rest, which you *must* do if you want to get stronger.

Even if you *have* the time, genetics, obsession and desire, you can always control the size of your muscles. To make muscles *smaller,* all you have to do is lift less weight. The other way to do it is train six days a week, two hours a day, and push yourself as hard as possible. Overtraining, ironically, also shrinks muscles. Very few women (or men) have any need to worry about getting too big.

With that myth broken, let's move on to reality. By now, you probably know that you *need* this thing called strength. Because strength training for women has gotten so much press in recent years, I won't belabor the benefits here. In short, stronger muscles help you:

- maintain a leaner body (The greater your percentage of muscle to fat, the speedier your metabolism becomes. This ultimately helps you burn fat faster.)

- have stronger bones and connective tissue

- stay active

- avoid injuries

- improve posture

- achieve better balanced muscle strength

- improve coordination

- decrease stress and improve self-image

- reduce the risk of falling and bone fractures as you get older

Although weight lifting in the 1990s was the number-one sport for women, who bought more than half of all gym memberships, women still have a problem staying with it. The average gym membership still lasts only three months. For every one woman who falls in love with strength training, there must be at least ten others who take a free training session when they join the gym and from that experience, do it a few times then don't come back.

To our credit, however, women have gotten much more active in the last two decades. We've become avid walkers, dancers, runners and skaters. Our legs and hearts are strong. But we're not such enthusiastic lifters, haulers, pullers and pushers because these things don't come easy for us. But as we get older, if we only do those lower body activities, we may find it very hard to lift children, groceries, furniture and suitcases. Preventing this doesn't take a *lot* of upper body strength work. Just a little often does the trick.

By now you might be saying, "Okay, so I'll do a little upper body work. Just tell me what and how often." I'll address those issues in the next segment.

But there's another issue that prevents a lot of women from pursuing strength—the gym, or, more specifically, the weight room.

It's unfortunate but true that few gyms are set up to inspire a "workout trance." Ideally, the atmosphere should be meditative, with music that invokes an inner journey—not blaring noise that dulls the senses. But this isn't the reality. So, as Muscle Yogini, you have three choices:

1. Block out your surroundings (wear earplugs or a Walkman or work with a trainer or friend who keeps your attention) and turn your mind within.

2. Buy your own equipment and work out at home.

3. Find classes you like, where you do exercises that fatigue your muscles with fewer than fifteen repetitions.

This last one is not so easy, since many "body-sculpting classes" involve high reps with light weights (and that disco music is meant to pump you up and dull your pain instead of taking you *into* your body and experience). Human nature is such that many women tend to keep lifting the same light weights in every class instead of even occasionally reaching for something heavier. Doing high reps with light weights is a muscle *endurance* activity. In other words, it doesn't strengthen muscles and bones and can be a waste of time. If you can lift a light weight for more than fifteen repetitions with ease (as people do in step classes or out walking with dumbbells), you're not strength training, you're doing aerobics. Using light weights this way arguably makes aerobic activity a bit more challenging but seldom strengthens the muscles. To do that, you have to do exercises that make your muscles steam, scream or fail between eight and fifteen reps.

In Praise of Shorter, Less Frequent Workouts

Like a lot of lifters, I used to overdo it. I trained four to six days a week, did between three to five sets (of eight to fifteen repetitions) per exercise and then rested a good thirty seconds to a minute between sets. This took about an hour and fifteen minutes per workout and my life was centered on training and eating. When I missed a workout, I felt crazed. This was not only exhausting, it wasted my time and energy and got me addicted to the "pump." Most people can only lift with gusto for about forty-five minutes. That's how long it takes to run out of "fuel" (stored carbohydrates—last night's dinner or this morning's breakfast). To get through a grueling work-out longer than that, you have to pump yourself up unnaturally with caffeine or carbo drinks to override your body's very sensible demand to stop. If you keep going on this way, day after day, eventually the muscles start to "eat themselves" for fuel (they become "catabolic"). Shorter workouts let you work *with* your body's energy, not against it. Therefore, you can work with intensity and still have time and energy left over for other things! (My strength workouts now last only twenty to forty-five minutes and I typically train only once or twice a week—either my whole body at once, or my upper and lower body on different days. I also get plenty of other supplemental strength work from teaching classes. If I weren't teaching, I'd still strength-train only twice a week.)

I didn't believe that I could get more from doing less, so it took me a while to get over my obsessive, inefficient approach. My friend and colleague Roger Schwab, owner of Main Line Health and Fitness and author of *Strength of a Woman: The Truth about Training the Female Body,* finally set me straight. Roger is a passionate advocate of twice-a-week, full-body, high-intensity work-outs with no rests between exercises, since this method strengthens muscles, bones and the cardiovascular system at one time and allows the body to work and rest as a whole. Roger convinced me that it's even better to train twice rather than three times a week since three sessions a week don't give the body adequate rest time. Training as I did, doing back and chest one day, legs the next, shoulders and arms on the third day and resting on the fourth day, before starting the cycle all over, doesn't work the same muscles on successive days. But the body goes into perpetual "repair mode" and therefore never fully rests. Unless you rest, you won't have enough energy to work with the intensity you need, and you won't improve.

Working with intensity doesn't mean lifting quickly. It still means lifting slowly and with good form while you take each set to extreme fatigue or muscle failure. Then, you quickly move on to the next exercise without resting.

If you work with this intensity, you need only *one set per exercise* and *one exercise per major muscle group*. For bigger muscles such as back, chest and legs, you may want to do two or three different exercises—but you still only need one set of each exercise. Doing these "one-set wonders" helps you put more effort into each set because psychologically it's easier to know you only have to do one of each. However, working this way doesn't work for everyone. Beginners can't always muster the intensity or endurance to commit to one good set. So if you're just starting, you may want to do two or three sets at a lower intensity for six weeks to three months. But you should soon aim for doing one set of each exercise at a higher intensity so you get more out of doing less.

Another Look at Sets and Reps

As for how many repetitions to do per exercise, there are standard and not so standard answers. The standard answer is this.

If you reach extreme muscle fatigue or failure after:

- 6 to 8 reps, you build "brute strength." (Power lifters use this technique with heavy weight.)

- 8 to 12 reps, you build muscle size. (This is the rep range bodybuilders prefer, using moderate weight, especially for the upper body.)

- 12 to 15 reps, you build muscle endurance but not size. (Endurance athletes like rowers and bicyclists often use this rep range, using light weight. However, bodybuilders occasionally use this rep range or higher for training legs or before a contest.)

These are time-honored, valid approaches. But there's a more intriguing way to reach fatigue: Instead of counting repetitions, time them, so that you *time the entire set.* In other words, put your muscles into contraction for set periods of time, according to the muscle group you're working. After all, muscles come in different sizes, with different amounts of muscle fibers that fatigue at different rates. Legs, back and chest muscles, for instance, take longer to fatigue than arms. It doesn't make sense, therefore, to work a large muscle group for the same amount of time as you'd work a small one. So, next time you work out, use a stopwatch. For instance, when you work:

- Buttocks (with squats, leg presses, deep pliés, etc.), your set should take 90 seconds to 2 minutes.

- Legs (with hamstring, quads, inner/outer thigh, etc.), your set should take 1 minute to 90 seconds.

- Back, chest and abdominals (with rows, chest presses, crunches, etc.), your set should take 45 to 75 seconds.

- Shoulders and arms (also calves and wrists) (with shoulder presses, biceps curls, triceps extensions, etc.), your set should last 45 seconds to 1 minute.

If you don't want to use a stopwatch, simply time the *duration* of each repetition and count it the old-fashioned way ("one banana, two banana, . . ."). All you have to do is choose how long you want each rep to last. For instance, if you want to do 10-second reps (they're the hardest because they keep you in contraction longer) while working buttocks for 90 seconds to 2 minutes, you'd do 9 to 12 reps. Don't think too hard about this. If you want to work slowly and intensely, simply copy down the following numbers and take them to your next workout.

To work your buttocks for 90 seconds to 2 minutes per set with:

10-second reps, do:	9 to 12 reps
8-second reps, do:	11 to 15 reps
6-second reps, do:	15 to 20 reps

To work your legs for 1 minute to 90 seconds per set with:

10-second reps, do:	6 to 9 reps
8-second reps, do:	8 to 11 reps
6-second reps, do:	10 to 15 reps

To work your back, chest and abdominals for 45 to 75 seconds per set with:

10-second reps, do:	5 to 8 reps
8-second reps, do:	6 to 9 reps
6-second reps, do:	8 to 13 reps

To work your shoulders and arms (and other small muscles like calves and wrists) for 45 seconds to 1 minute per set with:

10-second reps, do:	5 to 6 reps
8-second reps, do:	6 to 8 reps
6-second reps, do:	8 to 10 reps

Naturally, you don't have to be consistent and do all 10-second or all 6-second reps in one workout. Mix it up to suit yourself. However, when you are feeling particularly rushed, stressed, fatigued and impatient, doing 10-second reps can completely transform your mental state!

In Praise of Low-Tech Equipment

A painter has her palette, a singer has her songs, a poet has her vocabulary and a Muscle Yogini has her equipment—which can be anything at hand, from a broomstick to an expensive machine. In my opinion, the best, most enduring tools are low-tech. Dumbbells, bands or body weight alone have been the most popular equipment for years *because* they're so simple. They also promote a more organic form of body wisdom and leave you less dependent on a gym or machine.

All of these tools, however, have drawbacks. Working with body weight alone is easier to achieve with the legs and torso. You can get an intense lower body workout if you slow movements to a crawl, do deep pliés, squats, lunges and you combine these moves with yoga stretches and isometric holds. You can also work the torso muscles with body weight alone if you do balance exercises (you'll find some of these exercises in the yoga chapter, next). Working slowly and carefully with body weight alone can be even more effective than working quickly with weights.

But it's not so easy, especially for women, to gain *upper* body strength using only body weight. Push-ups, pull-ups and dips are tough to do unless you already have a base of strength, plus they can be hard on shoulders, elbows and wrists. Certain yoga poses like the Downward-facing Plank pose and Upward and Downward Dog (see the next chapter) build *some* upper body strength in big muscles like chest, back and abdominals. But they don't target smaller arm muscles, like triceps, as effectively as weight training can—and not everyone can do them. Plus, yoga postures generally employ *isometric* contractions rather than the *concentric* (shortening the muscle as you lift the weight) and *eccentric* (lengthening the muscle as you lower the weight) contractions of good old weight lifting. Isometrics are a valuable *secondary* way to get stronger. But they don't offer resistance through a full range of motion (the best way to get stronger) and therefore aren't as effective for building strength as full-range motions *with resistance.* You can get creative, however, and combine strength and yoga exercises. For instance, you can always add a few push-ups to a Downward-facing Plank pose.

You can work every muscle with dumbbells but ideally you should have a rack of different weights to address different-sized muscles. You also need to keep progressing and you can do this in a few ways:

- Use heavier weight, at least for a few repetitions, before finishing a set with lighter weight.

- Do different exercises.

- Use varying tempos (start the set with 10-second reps, for instance, and finish with 6-second reps).

- Switch the order of exercises (but it's best to work your big muscles first and smaller muscles last).

- Use half reps and holds in the most challenging parts of the motion (in other words, combine full and small range of motion moves and try just holding the weight for several seconds in an isometric contraction).

The main problem with dumbbells is they leave "dead zones" through which there's little or no resistance on the muscle at all. So you need to avoid those dead zones as much as possible—and avoid hurling the weights around too fast.

Weighted bars (like barbells but without the end plates) have been popular for a few years, especially in fitness classes. The problem with these is that they're relatively expensive and unless you can add weighted plates on the ends (which can get time-consuming and cumbersome), you get one weight and one weight only for every muscle group, which is too light for some and too heavy for others.

Elastic resistance bands have been around for a long time as rehab and strength tools. Flat latex strips, called Dyna-bands (also called Therabands) are still the cheapest and most effective and portable workout tools. Because bands are light, they let you work against the downward pull of gravity. In other words, you don't always have to lift from floor to ceiling to feel the resistance as you do with dumbbells and bars. This lets you pull bands on all sorts of angles. This is not a smart thing to do with free weights, since it stresses the joints. The main problem with bands is they can be uncomfortable to hold. Older people and people with wrist problems or arthritis usually have a hard time with the grip. Sport cords with handles solve this problem but are a little less versatile since the elastic cord is usually one set length. So if you want to change resistance with it, you inevitably have to hold a handle in one hand and the cord in another—not very comfortable. Another problem with elastic resistance is you never know *how much* you're lifting—whether you're using five pounds of force or ten, so you have to go by feel. But you can easily change resistance by "choking" up or releasing the band or by using two or three bands at once.

I like the **pole and band**, featured here because it offers resistance through a full range of motion, like an elastic band, yet gives you something solid to hold on to, like a weight. It's easy to adjust the resistance and feels more like a "real workout" and not just a second-rate substitute for a gym workout.

The pole and band offer several other advantages:

1. The pole is easy to control—easier than a free weight because you don't jerk the bar (the band holds your body steady).

2. On that same note, standing up and holding the torso steady while pulling on the band lets you feel your abdominal stabilizers working more effectively than when you're holding free weights. (Free weights tend to throw you around a bit more.)

3. You can change your level of resistance at any time by simply rolling or unrolling the band around the pole, without missing a rep. You don't have to put down one set of free weights and pick up another, load or unload plates or change the pin in a weight stack in the middle of a set.

4. Because the band and the pole are light, you can use angles that you can't use with a weight.

5. The equipment is versatile. You can use either the pole or the band alone.

6. It's portable. You can do your strength workout anywhere.

The main disadvantages with the pole and band are:

1. You need to *anchor one end of the band* somewhere on your body so you create a steady place to pull from. This isn't really a disadvantage unless you're doing standing exercises and are very tall. You can get inventive and loop the band around a post, bench or other fixed object (to do rows, lat pulls, etc.). Be aware, however, that you can rip the band on a sharp corner. So be advised and, if possible, shave or sandpaper any rough spots. (Should the band snap, however, the sound is usually more ferocious than the sting.)

2. Any pole or barbell distributes the weight between both arms but not always evenly. We tend to lift more with the stronger arm. That's why it's good to *address each limb individually.* Here, you can do that by using the band alone.

Working with the Pole and Band

The pole and band featured here are the P.R.O. bar and P.R.O. band, manufactured by Fitness Wholesale. (See "Resources" for more information on the variety of poles, bands and their different strengths, videos and where to order all of the above).

Do these exercises in the order presented here to work the large muscles first.

Be sure to limber up your muscles and joints before *doing this workout.* The Temple Dance form (see chapter 4) offers a very thorough warm-up option. Choose four to five postures or do the whole thing. Before beginning the pole workout, put the pole through the band loops and adjust the ends of the band so they're twelve to eighteen inches apart.

Work slowly! Take *at least* 4 seconds for each repetition. Be adventurous and try 6-, 8- and 10-second reps!

Work hard! If you can do your final reps with ease, roll the band tighter around the pole. If you can't maintain good form because the resistance is too great, unroll the band a bit. After finishing one set, move right into the next exercise without resting (but, remember, don't rush the exercises themselves). If an exercise feels too hard, skip it and try it another day. If it creates a burning in the muscles you're intending to work, you're probably doing it right. If you can't feel it, check your form or your resistance. If it causes sharp joint pain, especially on one side of the body, avoid it.

Try to maintain good posture throughout every exercise. To achieve this, hold your:

- Lower back in a slight arch

- Abdominal and lower back muscles in a slight contraction

- Chest lifted

- Shoulders down and back

- Neck long

- Knees "soft" (not bent or locked)

- Wrists straight (hold the pole with four fingers—no thumb, unless you're worried about dropping it; this will help you gain better control of your wrists)

The postural details may sound like a lot to remember. But once you "set" the posture in your muscles, it'll become automatic.

This workout should take approximately 20 to 25 minutes.

Do your pole and band or any strength workout twice *a week.* If you're also dancing and doing yoga, you're getting plenty of "secondary" strength work. Remember, muscles need time to rest.

A word on legs: This workout, as you'll see, features just one leg exercise. No, I don't think this is the only leg exercise you need. But if you have to choose one, it's a good one (so are wide second-position pliés) and you can use your pole with it. Since I've written extensively about leg exercises in my other books, I don't want to repeat all that information. Also, as I mentioned earlier, women favor workouts that strengthen the lower body and therefore we tend to have strong legs. I wanted to focus this section on a big missing piece—upper body strength.

A note on orientation as you train: We'll use the Movement Mandala here to help with placement. If you're already familiar with my approach to placement via the clock face, I hope this further clarifies and doesn't simply confuse you.

The Band and Pole Workout

1. Seated Row

Sit on the floor or a small step with knees bent, heels into the ground, toes flexed and band wrapped around feet. Take a slightly wider than shoulder-width grip on your pole. Palms are down. Roll the band around the pole so it rolls toward your ankles before you begin. Sit up straight (don't slump forward or lean back). Start this exercise in your back first. Pull your shoulder blades back and down, *then* pull your elbows behind your torso (keep elbows on a horizontal line) while you push the chest forward. Straighten the arms to release, and relax the back and shoulder muscles *without rounding the back forward.* In other words, sit tall throughout.

Works   The back muscles (the "lats," or latissimus dorsi muscles, which run from armpits to waist), also your upper back (the rhomboids) and your lower back as a stabilizer.

Direction	Pull the bar on a *horizontal* line. Or pull up toward the chest to an *upper diagonal*.
Be sure you	Keep a small arch in the lower back and push the chest forward as the pole touches your torso.
Oppositions	The chest pushes forward as back muscles squeeze and pull back.
Variations	Use a wide, overhand grip to stress upper back muscles. Use a narrow grip to stress the lats. (When you use a narrow grip, keep the pole traveling in a horizontal line—more effective for lats.)

2. *Flat Chest Press*

Stand up, step through the band and put the band at the height of a bra strap. Hold your pole in front of the nipple line. With hands shoulder-width apart, roll the pole toward yourself to tighten the band. Pole should touch the chest. Palms are down. Before you start, make these postural adjustments: pull shoulders down and back, lift your chest, hold in abdominals and soften knees. Now press the bar directly forward (to your north), parallel to the floor. As arms straighten, keep chest lifted, elbows slightly bent.

Works Chest (pectorals) and shoulders (front deltoids).

Direction Press the pole on the *horizontal* line.

Be sure you Keep the shoulders down and back to put less stress on the shoulders, more work in the chest. Don't collapse the chest or lock elbows.

Oppositions As arms extend forward, pull shoulders back (but don't lean back).

Variation ***Incline chest press.*** Press the pole up and forward on an upper diagonal. This emphasizes upper pectorals, the weakest part of the chest. Incline presses are harder but also give you more "cleavage." Avoid pressing the pole too high (avoid vertical), as this uses too much shoulder muscle and not enough chest. For a more complete chest workout, do one set "flat" and one "incline." Switch the order of inclines and flats with each workout.

Stand on the band. Tighten the band by rolling the pole down to your thighs. Take an overhand grip on the pole, hands shoulder-width apart. Before you start, make these postural adjustments: pull shoulders back and down, hold in abdominals and soften knees. Pull the pole up to your *chest only*. Pulling it higher (and using a narrow grip) uses the trapezius muscles in the upper back— not very pretty when developed on a woman. Pulling the bar up to the shoulders or chin can also stress the delicate shoulder rotators. As you lift the pole, check your form. Upper arms should be parallel to the floor; elbows are higher than wrists. Keep your wrists straight. Avoid shrugging shoulders as you pull the pole up. Remember to *slowly* lower the bar each time.

Works Shoulders (deltoids).

Direction Pull the pole directly up the *vertical* along your body (taking it too far out in front of you puts too much stress on the shoulder joints).

Keep the shoulders down as you lift the pole. Avoid arching the lower back.

Oppositions As you raise the pole, press shoulders and feet down. As you lower the pole, keep the chest lifting.

Variation If you *want* to work your trapezius muscles in the upper back, use a narrow grip.

4. Shoulder Press

When you lift the pole overhead, you put your lower back at risk. If you have any doubts about your lower back strength, skip this one and come back to it when you're stronger. Start by resting the bar on your chest, palms up, hands a little wider apart than shoulders. Press the pole overhead but avoid locking your elbows as you straighten the arms. This shoulder press, passing in *front* of the face, is much safer on delicate shoulder rotators than taking this or any bar behind your head.

Works	Shoulders (particularly the middle deltoid).
Direction	Press pole directly up the *vertical* (pushing it forward could stress shoulders and lower back).
Be sure you	Hold the torso steady as you lift the pole.
Oppositions	Pull shoulders down as you raise the arms.
Variation	Try various ranges of motion. Press the pole just up to your nose or just over your head. Believe it or not, these smaller ranges of motion, mixed with the full range of motion, make this exercise more challenging.

5. Biceps Curl

Lower your arms by your sides. Then roll the band and pole down your legs to tighten the band. Return to standing. Take a palm-up grip, arms shoulder-width apart. Bend the elbows to lift the pole. As you do this, squeeze the upper arms into your torso, as if you were holding a pencil under each armpit—and keep them there. This helps isolate the work in the biceps—not the shoulders.

Works Upper arms (biceps).

Direction Start with the arms down (on the *vertical*). Bend the elbows so the forearm ends up on the *upper diagonal.* Lifting the pole higher takes resistance off the biceps, which makes this less effective.

Be sure you Fix the upper arm into your torso to avoid moving elbows forward or back. Use abdominal strength to stabilize your lower back.

Oppositions As you curl the bar, press your feet down into the floor.

Variation *Reverse curls.* This variation targets forearms—also biceps. Unroll the band a bit and take a palm-down grip on the bar. The targeted muscles (forearms and biceps brachialis) are smaller and weaker than the biceps, so this is harder than regular biceps curls.

This is a welcome relief from curls. It's simple but surprisingly effective. Start with forearms horizontal (make sure you've got resistance on the band). Also make sure your torso feels solid. Arching the lower back is tempting here: Don't do it. If anything, "cheat" your weight forward a bit so you can't arch. Extend your arms forward on the horizontal line, as if presenting a tray of food.

Works	Biceps, shoulders (front deltoids) and torso stabilizers.
Direction	Keep the motion *horizontal*.
Be sure you	Use a range of motion you can control. The farther your arms go out away from your body, the harder it is on your back.
Oppositions	As you extend the arms forward, pull the abdominals back into your spine.
Variation	This *is* the variation on biceps curls.

This is a quirky exercise but it works on the triceps. The only problems are: the band can pull your hair, leave a red welt on your neck and, if the ends of the bands are too close, they can squish your breasts. So pull your hair to the side, throw a towel over your shoulders and widen the band to steer clear of your breasts. Put the band loop behind your neck so the pole hangs in front of you like a guitar. Then roll the pole up to your breastbone. You'll buy yourself a little more range of motion if you incline your torso slightly forward and bend your knees throughout. Take an overhand grip on the pole. Hands should be shoulder-width apart. Press the pole to your thighs. Keep wrists straight, especially at the bottom—this adds more muscle fibers into the movement (in a muscle that many women want firm).

Works Triceps—the back of the upper arm.

Direction Press from the *upper diagonal* down to the *vertical* line.

Be sure you Work through the full range of motion.

Oppositions As you press the pole down, lift the chest slightly up and forward.

Variation Take a palm-up grip. It's harder this way and it targets the outer head of the triceps muscle even more.

Band-Only Exercises

8. One-Arm Triceps Extension

This is a very effective exercise, even more so than the one above because it works all three heads of the triceps (press-downs mostly target two out of three). Remove the band from the pole and put the pole aside. Take the band in your right hand, lift it up overhead and grab the long end with your left. Anchor your left hand (with the band) on your left *hip* and pull the band taut (as you proceed, if you notice it's too tight or slack, make adjustments). Keep the lifted elbow steady and pointed to the ceiling the whole time. Don't let your upper arm dance around and *don't* let your right forearm rest on your head. Get that arm *behind* your head for a full range of motion. As you lift the arm, keep the wrist straight.

Works The back of the upper arms (all three heads of the triceps).

Direction Forearm begins on a *lower diagonal* and ends up on the *vertical.*

Be sure you Fix the upper arm so it doesn't move—and point the elbow directly up.

Opposition Pull the band down with your left hand as you extend the right.

Variation If you want to playfully test your balance and torso strength (in the spirit of the Muscle Yogini), stand on one leg while you perform this exercise. To give the triceps a good time try 8 full slow reps, followed by 8 half reps (with forearm lifting from lower to upper diagonal). Follow with 4 slow full reps. Yaa! Switch arms.

9. Rear Delt Pullback

This one's great for avoiding a slumped-over posture. Take an overhand grip on your band, directly in front of your chest. Make sure the band has tension even in a rested position (don't let it go slack). Again, adjust your form *before* you start: soften elbows and *fix* them in a slightly bent position. You don't want to lock elbows, as this puts stress on the elbow tendons (and not on shoulder muscles). On the other hand, don't bend the elbow during the exercise as this takes the work out of your shoulders (and puts it in the triceps, but not in a way that works them intelligently). In other words, if you lock or bend elbows, you cheat. Pull *only* from the rear part of the shoulder. Pull the band to your chest. Elbows end up slightly behind your shoulders. Keep wrists straight.

Works   Rear part of shoulder (rear deltoids).

Direction   Pull both the band and the arms on the *horizontal* line.

Be sure you   Fix elbows in a slightly bent position and keep shoulders down.

Opposition	Press chest forward as hands pull behind your torso.
Variation	***One-arm pullback.*** To double your workload, do one arm at a time. Keeping arms horizontal, fix your left arm in the NW corner. Pull the right arm from NE to SE. Switch arms.

The Perfect Squat

Of course, we had to have *one* leg exercise in here. So I chose the squat with a pole since using the pole helps perfect squat form. Many people still think of a squat as a "knee bend." It's really a "sit back," a hip action. The knees just go along for the ride. Using the pole as a balance stick helps you feel the counter-weight of your hips moving back. The stick not only gives you security but also keeps you from reaching your torso too far forward.

10. The Perfect Squat

Take a stance approximately 1½ times wider than your hips. Turn the left toes to 11 and right toes to 1 o'clock. Hold the pole with arms straight at your body's midline. As you sit your hips back, press your arms forward into the pole (but avoid shrugging your shoulders forward). At the bottom part of the squat, thighs are horizontal, parallel to the floor. Keep the weight in your heels and not in the balls of your feet. Keep the chin tucked down so that the neck is in line with the spine. Abdominals should press back into your spine. As you come up, press the heels into the floor and squeeze the buttocks.

Direction In a perfect squat, your torso will incline forward to an upper diagonal.

Be sure you Keep a slight arch in the lower back, press the chest forward and avoid sticking out your chin.

Opposition The pole helps you feel the opposition between hips sitting back and chest inclining forward.

Variation To make this move more challenging, lower down into a full squat but lift only halfway up. Do this very slowly. You can also do this with the pole on your shoulders, standing on the band. Theoretically, you're adding resistance, which will make the muscles work harder, but this variation has drawbacks. The band's resistance adds only minimal extra work for the legs. Meanwhile, the band also pulls the pole down on your spine, which compresses the vertebrae (a heavy weight compresses the spine even more). Add extra resistance or weight on your shoulders *only* if it doesn't bother your back. I prefer the pole-only version of this squat, with deeper, slower motions.

On-Your-Back Variations

Not everyone has the strength to perform standing exercises. Even those who do sometimes need to turn the world on a different angle to alleviate boredom, break bad habits, experience sensations from a different perspective or work around an injury. The following are all horizontal variations of exercises presented above. Keep the same form as I described earlier even though you're lying on a step or bench. These exercises do not have photographs to accompany them, so you have to use your mind's eye. All the same rules apply to the following exercises as explained in their standing variations.

11. Rows

Lying on a step or bench, extend one leg to the ceiling and put the other foot on the floor. You'll be more comfortable wearing shoes for this. Keep your knee of the lifted leg bent, flex the foot and place the band over your instep. Roll the pole toward your ankles so you start the exercise with resistance. Pull the pole to your breastbone, down the *vertical* line. You can also pull on a *lower diagonal,* from feet to your chest, to focus the work in your upper back. Whatever your choice, be sure to maintain a safe spinal position. Use your abdominal stabilizers to avoid wobbling in this position. As the pole touches the chest, squeeze shoulder blades together and lift the chest to the ceiling. Allow the elbows to drop below the bench.

12. Chest Press

Lie on a step or bench, with the band looped around your back, like a bra strap. Roll the pole and band close to your chest before you begin (so you start with resistance). Press the pole up on a *vertical* line for flat presses; to an *upper diagonal* over your head for incline presses; to an *upper diagonal* toward your belly button for decline presses. As you lower the pole to your chest, make sure your elbows move below the bench.

13. Biceps or Reverse Curl

Lie on the floor and extend your legs *almost* straight but keep knees slightly bent, heels pressing into the floor. Use abdominal strength to hold this position. Wrap the band around your feet and roll the pole down to your knees before you begin. Curl the pole up toward your chest. Your forearms begin on a *horizontal* and end on an *upper diagonal,* close to your chest. Make sure that elbows don't touch the floor as arms bend or straighten.

14. Half Upright Row

Lying on the floor, as above, pull the pole to your chest on a *horizontal* line. This variation is even better on the floor than standing because it's gentler on the lower back.

If you're truly limited to a horizontal position, you can also try the shoulder press, biceps tray exercise and triceps press-down while lying down. Be inventive. Be a Muscle Yogini!

Recap

An average number of repetitions per exercise is 8 to 12 for the upper body. However, you can apply the 6-, 8- and 10-second rep concept here and *time* your sets according to the size of the muscle group. The slower your reps, the fewer your reps. So more reps don't always mean harder work. The following rep range takes all of that into account.

Band and pole

1. Seated rows (wide or narrow)   5 to 13 reps
2. Chest presses (flat or incline)   5 to 13 reps
3. Half upright rows   5 to 12 reps
4. Shoulder presses   5 to 12 reps
5. Biceps curls   5 to 12 reps
6. Biceps tray exercise   5 to 12 reps
7. Triceps press-downs   5 to 12 reps

Band only

8. One-arm triceps extensions   5 to 12 reps
9. Rear delt pullbacks   5 to 12 reps

Pole only

10. Perfect Squats   9 to 20 reps

On-your-back variations

11. Rows   5 to 13 reps
12. Chest presses   5 to 13 reps
13. Biceps or reverse curls   5 to 12 reps
14. Half upright rows   5 to 12 reps

Now that you're on your way to becoming a Muscle Yogini, you'll take that same willingness to surrender to a workout trance into yoga—a much more seductive realm, the world of stillness within movement.

6 Woman-Power Yoga

Contrary to what many people think, the word *yoga* doesn't mean "to stretch." It roughly translates as "joining mind, body and spirit with God." It also means different things to different people. There are over a hundred forms of yoga—Hatha, Kundalini, Ashtanga, Iyengar and Bikram, to name just a few. All of these "physical yogas" help you breathe deeply, stretch your muscles, give better mobility in the joints, realign your posture, calm your mind, open your heart, soothe your spirit and regulate your hormones. There are also more *meditational* forms (Bhakti and Raja yoga are examples), which have no set movements at all. Regardless of whether your approach is purely physical, metaphysical or a blend of both, yoga can do many good things for your health. However, it's really not true yoga unless there's at least a glimmer of the Spirit in your practice.

What Yoga Does for the Spirit

Many eastern yogis say the real yoga is in the breath and not in the postures—and that our fixation on form and alignment is a mostly Western phenomenon. There's some truth to this. But the postures—especially those that are "kinesthetically safe and correct"—promote greater blood flow, better alignment and "functional" strength. Combined with deep breathing, the postures ease both mental and physical stress and help you redirect your thinking out of worry and into a loving regard for yourself and others. Done in this spirit, yoga teaches you compassion for your weaknesses and gives you faith in your progress. Mostly, yoga lets you pay exquisitely close attention to your posture and breathing, which is nothing short of a form of worship.

Yoga is one of the holiest of the movement arts *because* there's so much stillness in it—which inspires deep inner voyaging. In yoga, you may move from posture to posture but, arguably, the real "magic" appears as you surrender into a pose. In stillness, you can allow mental chatter, pain and tightness to disappear.

Yoga has been around for at least two thousand years. In the second century A.D., a man named Patanjali wrote and published the *Yoga Sutras.* This is *still* considered the ultimate "manual to higher consciousness" for people on the yoga path. Using little stories, or "sutras" (*sutra* means "thread" or "little story"), Patanjali outlined what he called the "Eight-Fold Path of Enlightenment." These aren't unlike the Twelve Steps of AA in that you can study each step over and over and always find something new. The steps *sound* simple but they should be called "The Eight Hardest Things You Could Ever Do." I mention them here because they take you into the *spirit* of Yoga.

Step 1. Take your attention off worldly distractions and focus inward. In yoga practice, you do this when you forget your outside life and put your attention on your breath and body. In other parts of your life, you do this when you distinguish between those things that may bring immediate pleasure (your desires) and those things that truly help your development as a spiritual being (your needs). Following step 1 doesn't mean you have to forsake all material desires. But its lesson is that while fame, sex, power, money, a flashy physique or whatever else you desire may bring many advantages, they aren't critical for *survival.*

Step 2. Practice nonattachment to outcomes both good and bad. In yoga practice, you follow step 2 when you don't judge your progress or compare yourself to others. In other parts of your life, you do this when you have to let go of someone or something and after perhaps suffering the pain of detachment, feel lighter and free. You also do this when you practice "right action" without concern for results or individual gain.

Step 3. Meditative postures. Putting your body into often uncomfortable positions prepares you for the many demands of life. *Asanas*, the Sanskrit word for "postures," also help you create new relationships with the discomfort, so you can handle tense situations with more grace and sit still in meditation without being distracted by your body.

Step 4. Regulate the breath. Yoga practice helps you breathe deeply and often! Many yoga teachers provide instruction in various forms of *pranayama* (the Sanskrit word for "breath"). According to the yoga tradition, these techniques (like inhaling through the nose and out the mouth, alternate nostril breathing or breathing with sound) not only help you inhale more oxygen but take in more "prana." (*Prana* is the Sanskrit word for "life energy"—called *chi* in the Chinese tradition, *ki* in the Japanese.) Regular deep breathing, in my opinion, works just as well as some of the fancier techniques.

Step 5. Turn your senses on and off. Mind-body communication takes many forms. Most of the time in yoga, you put your mind *into* your physical sensations. But there are times (when you're sweating through a particularly tough posture or getting your teeth drilled) when it's appropriate to send your mind *away*. Detaching yourself from pain can be useful in those occasional times. But you should always respect what pain is trying to tell you—especially a sharp, sudden pain that demands you stop. An experienced yogini learns when to put the mind fully into her sensations and when to pull it out. (Continued practice also helps you change your *perceptions* about what is painful.)

Step 6. Focus on an object *with* distractions. This is Meditation 101. This seemingly impossible task is to think of one thing only, notice when your mind wanders, then redirect your thoughts back to the original thought. Some of us never graduate from this course but I believe the attempt is more important than actually succeeding.

Step 7. Focusing on that object *without* distractions. This is advanced-level meditation. No distractions! I can't speak from experience here.

Step 8. Samadhi. This is roughly defined as merging with God or a higher self. This is enlightenment. I can't speak from experience here either—but I've had passing moments of great joy for no apparent reason.

Patanjali said that yoga helps quiet the mind so you can hear the "voice of God." In this state, your ego melts away and you no longer feel separate or different from other beings. You fall into a perpetual state of "in love," not with a romantic partner, but with life, with others, with God. You feel connected to all things because you realize you and all things *are* God.

Where the Subtle and Physical Bodies Connect: What Yoga Does for Chakras and Glands

Yoga affects both our physical and our subtle, or "energy," bodies. Just how and if these two bodies meet and interact remains somewhat of a mystery. The endocrine glands and the chakras, however, share common geography of the body. While the glands regulate hormone production and many other body functions, the chakras are believed to affect the energy, emotions and issues related to these areas. These things are thought to be related because hormones certainly determine how we feel, think and function, while our feelings, thoughts and energy affect which hormones we secrete.

Ayurvedic physicians (Ayurveda is the Indian ancient medical tradition) and metaphysicists have typically described chakras as little spinning wheels of consciousness. These "energy mandalas" are like funnels or tuners that receive subtle energy, then distribute this energy to different parts of the body along invisible pathways called *nadis* or meridians. Neither chakras nor nadis manifest in the physical body (although eastern medicine, particularly Chinese medicine, addresses the meridians as if they were in the body, with acupuncture and acupressure). Various schools of thought place chakras in front of, behind and inside the body. An "average" chakra is thought to be about two inches wide but gets bigger as a person's consciousness expands.

Although certain chakras and glands don't always line up precisely, they're often paired together because their "essence" is similar and their emotional and other issues often match. When a particular chakra is "shut down" or the energy is blocked, this is thought to be a precursor to disease. According to both Indian and Chinese medicine, health is the result of a balanced flow of energy through the whole body; blockages in the flow can cause physical, emotional, mental and/or spiritual stagnation. Stagnant energy is thought to be like a stagnant pool, affecting the body, emotions, mind and spirit.

Yoga postures that squeeze or stretch the glands (and other organs like the stomach, liver, etc.) not only promote a healthy flow of energy and stimulate the glands to secrete hormones, they bring awareness to the subtle energy centers connected to physical, spiritual, emotional and intellectual growth. Here's a brief introduction to your chakras and what they do.

1ST CHAKRA: THE ROOT CHAKRA.

This is the earthy, "grounding" chakra. Issues related to this chakra are mostly about survival, security and the will to live. This chakra also governs physical sensations associated with eating, movement and touch. A blocked first chakra can make you unaware of your own needs and keep you caught up in the struggle to survive. An open first chakra gives you a firm sense of who you are and helps you transcend your fear.

Where you find it: At the base of the spine.

Hormone connection: Adrenaline. Adrenal glands secrete stress hormones that help you fight or flee and also regulate fluid balance.

2ND CHAKRA: THE REGENERATIVE, OR PLEASURE, CHAKRA.

This watery chakra relates to sex and procreation but also symbolizes creativity in general. A blocked 2nd chakra may cause struggles with sexuality and creativity, which often leads to compulsive behavior. An open 2nd chakra creates comfort with sexuality and creativity—and helps you break out of old patterns where your energy feels blocked.

Where you find it: About four inches below the navel.

Hormone connection: The ovaries and testes secrete the sex hormones estrogen, progesterone and testosterone (which men and women all produce in varying amounts). In women, the 2nd chakra refers to both the uterus and the ovaries.

3RD CHAKRA: SOLAR PLEXUS, OR CENTER, CHAKRA.

Located in the digestive system, this chakra represents the fiery transformation of raw physical material (food) into energy. The 3rd chakra is also tied to our sense of identity. A blocked 3rd chakra can create arrogant or controlling behavior, also lethargy and depression. An open 3rd chakra creates genuine caring for others, good intuition and high energy.

Where you find it: Behind the navel.

Hormone connection: The pancreas controls glucose and insulin levels.

4TH CHAKRA: HEART CHAKRA.

This is the first of the "higher" chakras and where we feel affinity for others. Issues related to the 4th chakra move beyond the self and deal with human and divine love. A blocked 4th chakra can cut you off from your feelings and create fear of intimacy. An open 4th chakra increases your depth of life experience, brings compassion and expands the heart.

Where you find it: In your heart.

Hormone connection: The heart is an organ, not a gland. The thymus gland is associated with the 4th chakra. Hormones secreted here assist the immune system and regulate bone growth.

5TH CHAKRA: THROAT CHAKRA.

This chakra is about communication—not only verbal but also intuitive and telepathic. The 5th chakra is sometimes called a mouthpiece for the heart. It also colors the qualities of the breath, movement and sound and helps with practical intuition ("messages" that tell you, for example, to call a certain person). A blocked 5th chakra creates difficulty in all forms of self-expression. An open 5th chakra creates easy expression and a flood of messages, songs, phrases, poems and so on that apparently come from "nowhere."

Where you find it: At the base of the throat.

Hormone connection: The thyroid gland secretes hormones that regulate metabolism, brain, nerve and muscle function—also calcium levels in the blood.

6TH CHAKRA: BROW CHAKRA.

This chakra represents perception and intellect, also abstract intuition for bigger details beyond the practical. This is where intellect begins to merge with higher consciousness. A blocked 6th chakra makes people become "stuck in their heads," controlling and cut off from reality. An open 6th chakra creates a sense of living in harmony with inner and outer circumstances. It *is* possible to have an open 6th chakra and maintain a practical life, without getting too "spaced out."

Where you find it: Between your eyebrows.

Hormone connection: In some systems, the 6th chakra is connected to the pineal gland, in others the pituitary. I think it makes more sense to associate the pituitary gland here since it's closer to the frontal lobe and governs the entire endocrine system—especially the thyroid, adrenals and sex glands. The pineal seems to have been given a higher, special function all its own.

7TH CHAKRA: CROWN CHAKRA.

This chakra represents a pure state of consciousness beyond the worries of normal daily life. It's where we house our beliefs about God and the sacred. Psychic mediums also use it as the "meeting room" for spirit guides, angels, and so forth. This chakra is most often activated in meditation and dreams. When blocked, the spiritual life is cut off or suffers. When open, consciousness grows. Samadhi happens here.

Where you find it: In the pineal gland, behind the eyebrows (and behind the pituitary).

Hormone connection: The pineal gland secretes melatonin, which regulates sleep patterns according to light and darkness. The pineal also secretes a mysterious phosphorous salt, like tears, although scientists aren't sure what it does (could this be the nectar of spirit?). The pineal gland has also been called the "third eye" and "seat of the soul." Perhaps you won't be surprised to hear that it's bigger in children than adults, also bigger in women than men.

Back to Earth: What Yoga Does for Your Flesh and Bones

- Yoga relaxes and lengthens your muscles. Muscles contain "stretch receptors" which tell the nervous system if the body is tense or relaxed. Tight muscles send out a stress signal, which makes the adrenals pump adrenaline, cortisol and other stress hormones. Stress hormones aren't damaging in the short run (they help you steer clear of an accident, for instance) but constant stress exhausts the nervous system and leaves the body vulnerable to disease. Relaxed muscles, on the other hand, send out a "feel-good" signal, which then stimulates the brain to produce endorphins, serotonin and other chemicals of contentment.

- Yoga makes connective tissue stronger and more supple. Tendons and ligaments are the gristly bands that attach muscles to bones and each other. An injured tendon or ligament takes much longer to heal than a muscle since it's not elastic. In many cases, it's even better to break a bone than to injure connective tissue because bone can repair itself and even grow back stronger—connective tissue does not. Once pulled, connective tissue tends to stay loose and vulnerable for life. The good news is that when your muscles get strong, your connective tissue gets stronger, too (although this takes longer). A well-crafted yoga practice *should* make your connective tissue healthier. However, if you stretch too far or use bad form for years on end, you can permanently *damage* your connective tissue. The yoga postures presented in this book won't overstretch tendons and ligaments.

- Stretching sends nourishing oxygen into your cells and inspires better nerve function. This gives you more energy and strengthens your immune system.

- Yoga is good for the bones in two ways. First, the all-over weight-bearing postures strengthen bones in your upper and lower body. Second, yoga's calming effect on the mind decreases the amount of acid in the blood. A high acid content, caused by stress, robs the bones of calcium.

- Yoga can lower blood pressure. Inverted postures (when your hips are above your head) are especially helpful and offer immediate relief. When gravity sends blood into your neck and chest, this tricks your body into thinking that blood pressure has risen. Your body responds by dilating blood vessels, which immediately lowers pressure.

- Yoga makes you smarter and improves your memory! Although this sounds sensational, it's true. An overbusy brain acts like an overworked body. Performance suffers. Calming the mind with deep breathing and yoga improves brain function, which revitalizes even a middle-aged, faltering memory! (Hint: to improve your memory even more, avoid excessive amounts of alcohol; don't take sleeping pills; get a good night's sleep [getting up early helps]; take a multivitamin-mineral supplement with antioxidant vitamins A, C and E; avoid high-fat foods, which clog the blood flow to your brain, and, of course, move your body and engage your mind in exciting things.)

How Yoga Helps Women

From puberty to menopause, women's hormones are in a constant flux. Because yoga regulates the hormones, it helps us through every possible phase of our blood cycles: from PMS, menstruation and pregnancy into menopause and beyond. (For this reason, yoga would probably transport adolescent girls through puberty with greater ease but getting them to sit still isn't so easy. Plus, girls at this age need vigorous activity even more than yoga to strengthen their bones.) Yoga can balance our hormones through all these transitions but it helps to know which postures to use when. One posture can be great for PMS and menopause but counterproductive when menstruating or pregnant. Each posture in this book is marked accordingly, so you'll know when to use or avoid it. But first, here's an overview on how yoga affects hormones:

PMS. During the week or two before menstruation, estrogen drops and progesterone rises (see chapter 9, "Taming the Dragon"). Progesterone prepares the body for a possible pregnancy. It slows digestion and makes us weaker and more emotionally sensitive—the body's way of getting us to focus inward. The best postures for easing PMS symptoms are inverted postures (hips above head), lying-on-the-back postures, twists and supported forward bends. These stimulate the adrenal glands and the digestive and reproductive organs.

Menstruation. When you're bleeding, the flow of blood and energy moves down and out. It's best at this time to respect this agreement with gravity and avoid inverted postures that take the blood flow back *into* the body. Forward bends, slight back bends and postures on hands and knees with the chest higher than hips can ease cramps.

Menstruation is the body's "quiet time." Women are typically about 10 to 20 percent weaker at this time of month and would be wise to avoid any postures (or exercise) that feels too vigorous. Bleeding time is an opportunity to pull back, rest and prepare for the surge of energy that usually returns after menstruation. It's a time to favor long, slow and easy postures and moderate forms of exercise.

Menopause. I'm combining pre- or perimenopause (which can continue for *several years*), menopause (a nonevent, since it officially begins one year *after* your last period) and postmenopause. Yoga can ease many of the symptoms associated with these phases, especially mood swings and hot flashes. It also helps strengthen bones, which is important since bones typically deteriorate fastest two to three years after menopause (although bone loss slows down after that).

Although yoga isn't technically "aerobic," holding postures often increases blood flow in and out of the heart. (A steady aerobic practice, like dancing or fast walking, further strengthens the heart. Many teachers also combine yoga and aerobics in a nonstop hybrid of both activities.) Heart protection is important because after menopause, estrogen (which protects the heart) drops, which then triples a woman's risk for heart disease—equal to a man's risk. Yoga also soothes an *angry* heart—which doctors now suspect plays a critical role in creating heart disease.

Twists and forward bends are good for hormone rebalancing during menopause. Inverted postures are especially good for relieving hot flashes (they take the heat that would otherwise be rising to the skin and return it back into the body). Standing and more vigorous postures also help strengthen the heart and bones.

Pregnancy. Yoga is a wonderful, mostly stress-free way to exercise when pregnant. Yoga breathing exercises are similar to those taught in natural childbirth classes. Yoga doesn't guarantee an easy delivery. But it can help relieve pre- and postnatal discomfort.

How much yoga a woman should do throughout her term depends on her practice and fitness level *before* she got pregnant. If you are pregnant, pay attention to your body's feedback and don't do anything that feels strenuous. (If yoga or any exercise makes you start bleeding or leaves you exhausted, stop and call your doctor.) Naturally, you should check with your doctor before doing these or *any* exercises, especially if you're starting *while* pregnant.

Here are the main things you should know about doing yoga while pregnant:

- After your fourth month, don't lie on your back for more than three minutes. The weight of the baby's body in this position interrupts blood flow into the uterus, lowers blood pressure and reduces the amount of blood your heart pumps out. You can do all the on-your-back exercises with your torso propped up with pillows (as if reading in bed). Postures that put you on your side are good (lying on your left side is especially good since it eases blood flow into the uterus.)

- All exercises on hands and knees are good for the baby since gravity directs blood into the uterus. This position also tends to soothe lower back pain. The main drawback is it can be tough on wrists. If this is the case, lower down to your elbows.

- *Simple* standing postures help you adjust to your ever-shifting center of gravity. However, you should avoid *difficult* postures in case you lose your balance and fall. Avoid any risk of trauma to the abdominal area.

- Never take a yoga or *any* stretch too far when pregnant. The hormone relaxin, which helps your hips expand for birth, makes *all* your joints easily stretched and vulnerable. Relaxin can stay in your system for up to a year after giving birth. So be careful for several months after delivery.

- If you have varicose veins, some seated postures with legs crossed can impede blood flow into your legs and make the condition worse. However, some seated positions, like the modified squat, can improve blood flow. (Dancing, walking and cycling also get the leg blood flowing!) To avoid getting varicose veins or making them worse, you need to change your relationship with gravity more frequently. Standing still makes the blood pool in the legs. If you have to stand for long periods of time (washing dishes, giving haircuts, etc.), stand with one leg elevated on a stool. Switch legs.

- Immediately after delivery, you can begin exercising again with some deep belly breathing, gentle on-your-back stretches and an easy all-fours exercise like the Cat and Cow (also Kegels—internal vaginal squeezes). But you should wait until *after* your six-week checkup (longer if you had a C-section) before doing the more vigorous postures or exercises unless you feel very comfortable doing them.

Yoga's Dark Side

As wonderful as yoga is, like many good things, it has a shadow. Since yoga is such an ancient, honored tradition, some of its most ardent practitioners have been reluctant to update the postures to comply with guidelines of traditional modern exercise. Anyone who takes both Western fitness classes and yoga might run into two contradictory sets of rules. In fitness classes, for instance, straight-legged toe touches, leaning forward with a flat back without supporting your hands on something and the Plough (lying on your back with feet over head) were banned in the early 1980s. However, many yoga teachers not only use these postures but insist their students get into them as well. Adding *slight* modifications, like bending the knees or holding on to a support, can make risky postures safer and more satisfying.

Still, many yoga postures border on the absurd—even for the very fit. I bought a *beginner's* Ashtanga video not too long ago and could barely do one posture—and I'm fairly strong and flexible. The transitions between moves were extremely fast and dangerous even for people with exceptionally good body awareness. The teacher also only referred to the postures in Sanskrit (a beautiful language, but adding English names would have prevented me from craning my neck to see the TV screen). No wonder people find yoga intimidating!

When I was a full-time personal trainer, I trained several clients who had become "yoga casualties." Years of bad yoga practice had put extreme stress on their joints but very little in their muscles. So they ended up with weak muscles, overstretched connective tissue, "wobbly" joints and bad alignment, which left them vulnerable to injury and arthritis. Strength training corrected these problems. But some of the problems could have been avoided if the positions had opened the joints *less* and worked and stretched the muscles more. Opening the joints is fine but only after there's some base of strength in the muscles to support them.

Another common problem with yoga is that there can be too much going on at one time in a complicated posture. People often don't know where to put their focus—and therefore can't make intelligent modifications. For instance, most people can't do a Downward Dog with straight arms and legs, heels down *and* a long, slightly arched spine. The most important part of this posture is the back stretch—not the back-of-the-leg stretch. But many people straighten the legs and then round (compromise) their spines. An easy way to correct this is to bend the knees and lift the heels. Then, over time, as back flexibility increases, you can lower the heels to the floor to add the hamstring stretch. If you try to do it all at once, you end up doing nothing very well.

Complex postures have their place, if you're advanced in your practice. Complex postures use more muscles, make you breathe more deeply and enrich your experience. But, if there's a less stressful way to achieve a similar or even *better* end, why not use it? The yoga presented here has been simplified to make it user-friendly.

Some Practical Details

Warm up before you stretch. Warm muscles stretch further. Cold ones get injured more easily. A gentle, rhythmic warm-up sends blood into your muscles. The Temple Dance form in chapter 4, or part of it, is a good yoga warm-up.

Don't do yoga in a cold room for the same reasons listed above. If you must do yoga in the cold, wear many layers.

Some yoga studios heat the room to about 102 degrees Fahrenheit, which makes you sweat like crazy and releases every toxin (real or imagined) known to humans. (There's much debate between the medical and more mystical communities about what toxins are and if they exist.) Bikram Choudhury, the creator of Bikram yoga (known as the "yogi to the stars"), started the hot room practice. Now many studios offer "hot yoga." The heat helps you stretch into new dimensions. Hot yoga on a cold winter day is a great cheap vacation. But it's not advised for pregnant women or people with multiple sclerosis or heart conditions—all of whom need to avoid overheating.

Move thoughtfully into that good stretch. Many "power" and "aerobic" yoga classes push you fast between postures. This is fine if you know what you're doing. But if you're a beginner, you should do yoga slowly. Once you understand the fine points, then move faster. But even when you move quickly, "think slowly" so you can fully "inhabit" each position.

Hold that stretch. To get the most mileage from a posture, hold each position for at least ten seconds to thirty seconds. The American College of Sports Medicine recently released new exercise guidelines, recommending stretching two to three times a week to maintain fitness. Their research results noted lasting improvements in flexibility when people held stretches for that length of time—but minimal additional benefits when they held stretches for thirty to sixty seconds. Holding stretches for longer than a minute can compromise the connective tissue if the posture is unsafe or unsupported. If the posture is comfortable, there's nothing wrong with holding postures this long. But it's more a form of meditation than good medicine for the muscles.

Add reps! There's no cosmic law that says you can't combine strength training with yoga. Once you get into postures that are suited for it, try adding a few repetitions (i.e., push-ups, triceps dips, etc.) then hold your pose again. Try *partial* reps before you do full reps. Aim for four to twelve SLOW repetitions. The postures most suited for reps are the Cow and Cat and Downward-facing Plank pose (both for push-ups), the Half Lotus Sit (for triceps dips) and the Downward Dog (for shoulder presses).

Don't push it. A yoga stretch should straddle the border between pleasure and pain. If it hurts too much, back off. Never force a stretch (that's how you pull muscles and connective tissue). Move to the point of slight tightness and hold it there. Exhale to "surrender" into a deeper stretch.

Gaze inward. Once you understand a posture from the outside, focus *into* your body.

If you have the time, repeat each posture two to four times. The American

College of Sports Medicine recommends repeating each stretch four times to make maximum improvements in flexibility. Although this isn't always time-efficient or practical, it's a good idea when you want to focus on particularly tight areas. A word of caution: If you're stretching one leg or one side at a time, be sure to do the posture for the other side before repeating the stretch on the first side. (Otherwise, by the time you get to your second leg, you could be too tired, too stretched or out of time.) If repeating a series on one leg, however (as we do many times here), finish the series on both legs, before repeating.

Use all the help you need. Pillows, poles, straps, chairs and balls are all great yoga tools. In the following movements, you'll use a balance pole for standing stretches and a pillow for two postures. You can use the same pole you used in the strength exercises (see "Resources" for more on poles). Your pillow should be at least eighteen inches square, firm and four to eight inches high.

Invest in a sticky mat. This mat's different from a regular exercise mat since it won't skid across a wooden floor. It's very important to know that you can do a posture without slipping. You can find sticky mats in many sporting goods stores and yoga supply catalogues (check "Resources" in the back of this book). You can also do yoga comfortably *without* a mat on a carpet or sandy beach.

Breathing. Breathe normally and deeply through your nose. Exhale through your mouth as you stretch further. Keep a constant flow of breath running through the entire body (imagine it moving down into your fingers and toes). Avoid tensing your throat or belly.

Sounding. Chanting in various postures is a very powerful healer and leaves you buzzing! You can use all sorts of sounds. I like "ahm" because this sound is linked to the seven chakras. Each chakra has a corresponding sound, listed below; pronounce them so they all rhyme with "ahm." Frankly, I get them confused so I use "ahm" for them all and "Om" for seated meditation.

If you want to use specific sounds for specific chakras, try these:

1st chakra Lam

2nd chakra Vam

3rd chakra Ram

4th chakra Yam

5th chakra Ham

6th chakra Om

7th chakra Om or silence

The mind. Respect sudden pain and get out of any posture that causes it; but remain open to changing your opinion about *minor* discomfort. Use your mind to fully experience the subtlest and deepest sensations or, when it helps you endure, send your mind elsewhere.

The spirit. This may sound sentimental but be happy in each posture. "Smile down" into your organs, chakras, muscles and connective tissue. Don't judge your performance. When you do yoga, think of it as making love to your body in a slow, sensual, careful way.

Do these postures in sequence when linked in a group. They were designed to flow from one to the next. However, feel free to skip over difficult postures.

A final word on "my yoga." This style mostly draws on Hatha yoga with some influences from Iyengar and Ashtanga. Some are traditional postures with a difference. Others combine the stretches, alignment and sensibility of dance with yoga. The dancer's approach makes placement very precise and lends the postures a pleasing aesthetic both inside and out. Some of the postures also contain influences from the work of the late Joseph Pilates (pronounced "puh-LAH-tees").

The Pilates Method aims to strengthen and lengthen the muscles of the torso (the abdominals, shoulders, hips, upper and lower back), using subtle movements that improve alignment and maintain a stable yet supple spine. Pilates started creating his work back in the 1920s. A self-trained athlete, he created rehab exercises for hospital patients (using bedsprings, cords and other devices to help them build strength) and later worked with famous dancers, athletes and actors before his death in 1967. Although Pilates' work is often associated with some of his odd-looking equipment—the Reformer (which looks like a big mousetrap) and the Cadillac (which looks like a big cage)—it also contains a huge series of mat exercises. Those are the ones that have influenced me here.

I didn't set out to build a yoga practice based on the Pilates Method. I've actually been using some of these concepts for years, especially "centering," the alignment and pulling in two opposite directions. (Pilates himself incorporated yoga postures in his work.) But, after studying Pilates in more detail, I've learned a new appreciation for the power of the subtle torso motions he created and so must tip my hat to the master. However, like many forms of movement, his method is open to interpretation and so I use those things that make the most sense to me. Keep in mind, you won't be learning a traditional Pilates workout. You'll learn yoga with the sensibility of Pilates embedded in the form.

This yoga was created for people of "average" fitness. You don't have to be very strong or hyperflexible to begin this style although I wouldn't recommend this to senior citizens with no exercise experience. But if you start your yoga practice at least in your forties or fifties, there's no reason why you can't do all of these postures when you're eighty years old. Remember to get into each posture step-by-step and, as always, when a posture feels too hard, skip it or stop.

Standing Postures

These two series of standing postures are moderately challenging. I like to do them first (after a warm-up) to get the hard stuff out of the way—and end class on the floor. However, you may put them wherever you like.

THE PARALLEL LEG SERIES

Do postures 1, 2, 3 and 4 for one leg before repeating this series on the other leg.

1. Quad Stretch with Pole

Hold the pole in your left hand. Lift and hold your right foot in your right hand. Be sure to sink down slightly into your left supporting leg (balance on the center of your left foot). Pull the right foot *away* from buttocks and press your right hip forward. This stabilizes your lower back and stretches your right hip flexor. Lift your chest as you hold your balance and use your abdominal muscles to hold the torso upright.

Movement Mandala	As you face north, pull the foot to the south (not up the vertical line). Keep the torso and head aligned on the vertical axis.
Oppositions	As you pull the foot back, press the hip flexor and chest forward. Press the supporting foot down into the floor and lift up through the top of the head.
Works	Quadriceps, torso and pelvic stabilizers of the supporting leg.
Stretches	Quadriceps and hip flexor of the lifted leg.

Variation	If you can't pull your foot back very far, hold the knees together.
Avoid	Arching your lower back.
Organ and chakra connection	Anchor your weight in your tailbone (this puts awareness in your 1st chakra—which can stimulate the adrenal glands). Hold in the abdominal muscles to compress ovaries (2nd chakra) and digestive organs (3rd chakra) while you expand your chest and "open" your heart (4th chakra).
Especially good during	PMS and menopause because it helps you feel strong, balanced and revitalized. However, its hormonal benefits are more indirect than direct.
Avoid during	Pregnancy and menstruation if you don't have the strength or balance to do this.
Transition to the next posture	Bend the supporting knee further to prepare for the next move. Slowly start to incline the torso forward.

2. Inclined Pulling Bow Pose

Keep your spine in neutral alignment (don't excessively arch or round your lower back) as you incline the torso to an upper diagonal or further into a horizontal. This position releases the hip flexor and allows you to pull the foot both up toward the ceiling and back into your hand. Be sure to keep the chest and both hip bones facing the floor (i.e., don't open the hips to the side or twist your torso).

Movement Mandala	Incline the torso forward on an upper diagonal or horizontal. Keep pressing the foot back into your hand as you also lift the foot up to the vertical.
Oppositions	Pull the foot up and press down into your supporting leg. Also, press the foot back into your hand and press the chest forward.
Works	Supporting leg, back of torso and shoulder.
Stretches	Hip flexor of the stretched leg, front of torso and shoulder.
Variation	Incline only the slightest bit forward and hold the foot in both hands (very challenging).
Avoid	Twisting your torso or "opening" your hip to the side (do not imitate a dog over a hydrant).
Organ and chakra connections	The inclined torso stimulates both ovaries and digestive organs (1st and 2nd chakras) and further opens the heart (4th chakra).
Especially good during	PMS and menopause—even more so than the previous posture since it more directly stimulates the 2nd chakra.
Avoid during	Pregnancy and menstruation if you don't have the strength or balance to do this.
Transition to the next posture	Come back to a vertical standing posture and reach your right leg behind you. Keep your left knee bent.

Hold the pole in both hands for balance and to stretch your back muscles (or hold it in your left hand if you want a deeper stretch along the left side of your torso). Put your right leg behind the left (feet are as wide apart as hips). Keep both knees bent as you sit *back* into your hips. *Arch* (don't round) your lower back slightly (try to lift your tailbone to the ceiling). Focus on stretching the back of your left leg. If you don't feel this, shift your weight more onto that back leg. If you want to deepen the hamstring stretch on the front leg, flex your front foot. Lean only as far forward with a "flat" back as your hamstring flexibility will allow.

Movement Mandala Reach the head and arms north, torso to an upper diagonal. Sit hips back to the south.

Oppositions Hips press back as torso, head, arms pull forward.

Works Quadriceps, hip and torso stabilizers.

Stretches Hamstrings, buttocks and back.

Variation Straighten your front leg completely and flex your front foot to lift toes off the floor. Sit your front hip back to get the hamstring stretch.

Organ and chakra connection	This is a modified forward bend. Forward bends put gentle pressure on the sexual and digestive organs. Coming out of this position sends a soothing and rejuvenating fresh flow of blood to these areas (2nd and 3rd chakras).
Avoid	Rounding your back or locking your front knee.
Especially good during	Menstruation and pregnancy. This forward bend position can ease menstrual cramps and backaches. Also fine for PMS and menopause.
Avoid during	Okay at all times.
Transition to the next posture	Return to a vertical posture. Angle the bottom of the pole away from you so you can push it slightly forward during the Balance Pose. Set the pole in line with the center of your body.

4. Balance Pose

This is the hardest yoga posture. Feel your way into it slowly (and be sure you read the above transition). First, center your weight on the *ball* of your left foot. Make sure your left supporting knee is bent (the leg can be parallel or slightly turned out). Carefully incline your chest forward as you lift your back leg. Press into the pole for balance. Try to create a straight line from fingertips to heel, regardless of whether your "line" is horizontal or diagonal. Keep your head *above* your hips or, if you can stretch further, in line with hips (not below).

Movement Mandala	Pitch the head and chest north (on an upper diagonal or full horizontal) while you extend the leg to the south (on a lower diagonal or full horizontal).
Oppositions	Reach the chest and head forward as you lift the leg up (pull it away in the opposite direction). Your upper and lower body balance on your supporting leg like a seesaw. Press down into your supporting leg and lift up the abdominals.
Works	Abdominal and hip stabilizers, also quads.
Stretches	Torso, chest and hip flexor.
Variation	To make this easier, incline only slightly forward. To make this harder, don't use the pole. Try it with both arms above your back (and parallel to the floor), like half-folded wings by your sides.
Avoid	Arching your lower back. Don't try to break impressive stretch records with this either. Holding the balance is the exercise.
Organ and chakra connection	Open the chest and heart (4th chakra) as you incline forward. Your balance point is actually in your solar plexus (3rd chakra). Keep an awareness of the energy running through the whole spine, from the tailbone to the top of the head (and therefore through all the chakras).
Especially good during	PMS and menopause (good for creating balance when you might not feel grounded).
Avoid during	Menstruation and especially pregnancy. This is a tough pose to do when you're weak from menstruation or pregnant and front-heavy.
Transition to the next posture	Lower the right leg and stand up straight. Switch the pole into your right hand and start again from the top, lifting the left leg this time. If you're doing more than one set per leg, be sure to do the same four exercises on the other leg before repeating.

Do postures 5, 6 and 7 on one leg before changing legs.

5. *The Knee Hold*

Hold the pole in your left hand for balance. Bend your supporting knee as you pull the right knee to the chest. (Hold *under* the knee.) Next, open your right leg to the east or northeast and straighten your supporting leg at the same time. To find your balance, pull your torso up and slightly to the left. Your lifted leg provides counterbalance.

Movement Mandala First, draw the right knee up the vertical so it faces north. Then open the hip so that the knee turns east or northeast (depending on your flexibility).

Oppositions Knee lifts up and then slightly out in one direction. Torso pulls in the other direction. Press the supporting leg down and lift the head up.

Works Torso and pelvic stabilizers.

Stretches Hip flexor and inner thigh.

Variation	If opening the leg to the side is too difficult, you can do this holding your leg parallel (not turned out at the hip). But the parallel variation only stretches the lower back and buttocks—different muscles from the turned-out version.
Avoid	Leaning too far to the side with your torso.
Organ and chakra connection	This posture lets you "reset" your posture on a slight angle. To maintain this posture, imagine closing a zipper that runs from tailbone to the top of the head. Thus, you can think of it as a "chakra tune-up." Start with the 1st chakra at the base of the spine and draw the energy up through all other chakras.
Especially good during	PMS and menopause. Helps you focus and balance. Also eases backache.
Avoid during	Menstruation and pregnancy if feeling weak or wobbly.
Transition to the next posture	To prepare for the next move, slide your pole out farther to your left.

6. Karate Pose

Turn the foot of your supporting left leg to the northwest and bend that knee. Hold onto the right, lifted leg with your hand under the thigh (hold it from the back). Extend the leg so the hip opens and the knee faces the front (not the ceiling). The extended leg doesn't have to lift too high. Incline your torso away from the leg. Use your abdominal strength for balance.

Movement Mandala	Reach the leg to the east, torso to the west. If you're not very flexible, keep your leg horizontal or on a lower diagonal and your torso more on an upper diagonal. If flexible, try to lift leg and torso closer to upper diagonals.
Oppositions	Reach in opposite directions all the way through fingers and toes.
Works	Thigh muscles, torso and pelvic stabilizers.
Stretches	Inner thigh of lifted leg and torso.
Variation	If lifting the leg is too hard, simply incline the torso toward the pole and extend the leg out to the side, keeping the foot on the floor. This stretches the outer hip.
Avoid	Arching or rounding your back (that'll make you fall over) and don't lift the leg too high.
Organ and chakra connection	This posture emphasizes the solar plexus as your balance point. Thus there is a connection to the 3rd chakra—but its hormonal benefits are indirect.
Especially good during	PMS or menopause but only if you're up for it.
Avoid during	Pregnancy. With an expanding center of balance, it's too hard. Avoid during menstruation if feeling weak or wobbly.
Transition to the next posture	Move the pole farther away from your body.

Slowly incline your torso closer to an upper diagonal or horizontal if it's not there already. Keep your chest facing front as you align your torso and leg in a continuous line. After you find your balance, lift the top arm straight up the vertical. Keep your energy reaching up through the arm, down through the supporting leg. Then, slowly, lower that arm toward the pole (overhead on an upper diagonal or horizontal) and balance. Switch your focus to reaching the lifted leg in one direction and the top arm in the other. An easy way to get out of this posture is to turn your chest toward the ground, lower your leg and "fold" your body into a semisquat position.

Movement Mandala   Take your leg east; torso west (as you lift your right leg). Form a horizontal or continuous diagonal line with the leg and torso. Begin by lifting the free arm up the vertical and end by extending that arm overhead so it's on an upper diagonal or horizontal.

Oppositions	Begin reaching up through the extended arm and down into the supporting leg. As you lift the top arm to a diagonal or horizontal, reach away with your lifted leg.
Works	Torso and pelvic stabilizers.
Stretches	Hip, shoulder, chest.
Variation	If lifting the leg at all is too challenging, keep the foot on the floor and simply incline the torso to the side (supporting yourself on the pole).
Avoid	Opening the chest to the ceiling unless you are super flexible and strong in your torso.
Organ and chakra connection	This posture also balances on the solar plexus (3rd chakra). Put your focus there.
Especially good during	PMS or menopause if you're up for it.
Avoid during	Pregnancy. With an expanding center of balance, this one's too hard. Avoid during menstruation if feeling weak or wobbly.
Transition to the next posture	Sit on the floor.

Seated Postures

Do each of the following postures first on one side, then on the other, unless otherwise indicated.

The accompanying photos feature two women, sometimes representing two variations of one posture, both parts of a two-part posture or two separate moves. Each is indicated accordingly. As always, do whatever posture works for you.

Back Stretch (B)   Staff Pose (A)

Sit up straight, balancing on your "sit" bones. Extend your legs to the north; bend one knee so the heel (not the soles of your feet) rests on the floor. Straighten the other leg and flex the foot. Place your arms behind you and press fingertips into the floor to open the chest. Incline the torso slightly forward, without rounding the shoulders (A). Change legs and repeat on the other side. To stretch the spine, bend both knees and rest your chest on your thighs. Cross your wrists to stretch your upper back and shoulders (B).

Movement Mandala Staff pose—maintaining a mostly vertical spine, straighten one leg to the north and flex the foot. Bend the other leg so that your knee and toes point to the vertical. Incline the chest forward to an upper diagonal. Press the hands down on a lower diagonal. Torso inclines to an upper diagonal. Back Stretch—bend the knees so upper and lower legs form diagonals.

Oppositions Staff pose—chest pushes forward, hands press back. Shoulders and tailbone press down while head lifts up. Pull the toes of the flexed leg toward you and press the heel out. Back Stretch—point your head and tailbone down the vertical. Pull your navel up the vertical.

Works	Staff pose—torso stabilizers, quadriceps. Back Stretch—abdominals (hold them in).
Stretches	Staff pose—hamstring, chest, and front of shoulders. Back Stretch—entire spine.
Variation	If you're very flexible, try the Staff pose with both legs straight, both heels lifted, both thighs flexed.
Avoid	Rounding your back or straining your neck on the Staff pose.
Organ and chakra connection	The forward bend in both postures stimulates sexual and digestive organs (2nd and 3rd chakras).
Especially good during	PMS, menstruation and menopause (all forward bends are good for these). Add a pillow on your lap to relieve cramps.
Avoid during	Pregnancy. This forward bend is too restrictive for a growing belly if you keep one knee elevated to the front. Try this with legs slightly open to the sides.
Transition to the next posture	Repeat the Staff pose with the other leg straight, do the Back Stretch, then sit up straight again and take arms behind your torso.

Do postures 9 and 10 in succession before switching legs.

9. Upward-facing Plank Pose

Sitting upright, place your hands on the floor, behind your hips. Point fingertips toward your feet and bend your elbows slightly. Put both feet flat on the floor and rise up into a tabletop position (A). If this bothers your wrists, rest on your elbows (B). Keep your neck in line with your spine as if resting your head on a low table (don't throw your head back). Extend your right leg straight, parallel to the floor. For a hip flexor stretch, lower that leg until the foot touches the floor. Lift hips, buttocks, navel and shoulders to the vertical. Squeeze the buttocks to support your spine.

Movement Mandala Align your head, torso, and leg on a horizontal. To add a hip flexor stretch, lower the leg to a lower diagonal.

Opposition Reach up and out through the top of the head—and out through the lifted leg in the other direction, when it's horizontal. As you lower the leg, press hips, buttocks, navel and chest up.

Works Shoulders, arms, lower back and supporting leg.

Stretches Abdominals and hip flexor.

Variation If you can do the Upward-facing Plank pose on your hands with ease, straighten both legs and put both feet on the floor (very challenging!).

Avoid Dropping your head back.

Organ and chakra connection The chest and hips constantly lift up throughout this posture. Therefore, this emphasizes the heart (4th chakra) and sexual organs (2nd chakra).

Especially good during Menstruation. Just make sure your chest stays above your hips. Also fine for easing PMS and menopausal symptoms.

Avoid during Pregnancy, since this posture restricts blood flow into the uterus.

Transition to the next posture Cross the right ankle on the left knee.

Half Lotus Sit (A)   Buttocks Stretch (B)

Bend your elbows and lower your hips toward the floor but keep hips suspended. Slide your hips toward your heels to stretch outer hips and lower back. Keep chest lifted and shoulders pulling back and down (A). To deepen the stretch, sit the buttocks down, pull both knees up to the chest and rest on your elbows (B).

Movement Mandala   Hips lower down the vertical, then slide horizontally toward your feet with hips suspended. With hips down, knees pull up to an upper diagonal.

Oppositions   Half Lotus—as you suspend your hips off the ground, lift the chest. Shoulders pull down and back and the chin tucks down and in, to lengthen the back of the neck. Buttocks Stretch—as you pull the knees in, keep lifting the chest to avoid collapsing your spine.

Works   Half Lotus—upper back, abdominals, arms and supporting leg. Buttocks Stretch—abdominal and back stabilizers.

Stretches   Half Lotus—buttocks, hip rotators, lower back and chest. Buttocks Stretch—buttocks, hip rotators and lower back.

Variation   If the turned-out hip feels too tight, cross your legs so knees are closer together. That'll minimize the stretch.

Avoid   Shrugging your shoulders as you hold yourself up.

Organ and chakra connection	The Half Lotus Sit emphasizes the heart (4th chakra). The Buttocks Stretch also uses an open heart and stimulates the sexual and digestive organs (2nd and 3rd chakras).
Especially good during	Menstruation, for easing menstrual cramps. Also relieves PMS and menopausal symptoms.
Avoid during	Pregnancy. This exercise is safe to do during pregnancy but your belly might get in the way late in your pregnancy.
Transition to the next posture	Reestablish yourself in a seated, upright posture.

11. Boat Pose Variations

(B)   Boat Pose Variations   (A)

Incline your torso back and lift your chest to create a V shape (not a C shape) with your spine. Put your feet on the floor. This is your fail-safe position. Always return to this position if in danger of rounding or rolling onto your back. Lift the right leg so the shin is parallel to the floor, then lift the left in the same position (easing into it this way will keep you from falling backward). Lift the arms parallel to the floor (A). If you want to make this more challenging, straighten both legs and arms on an upper diagonal (B).

Movement Mandala For both variations—incline your torso back on an upper diagonal. Begin by lifting legs and arms horizontal, then, if you wish, move them to the upper diagonal.

Oppositions	Lift the chest up and pull the tailbone down. Abdominals and lower back push in and meet in the spine. As you extend the arms forward, pull the shoulders back. As you extend the legs up, pull the hips down. Keep the neck long and lifted throughout. Pull the ears up and tuck the chin slightly under.
Works	Abdominals, lower back, shoulders and quadriceps. These muscles work isometrically during this balancing exercise.
Stretches	Chest and hamstrings.
Variation	If you can't hold this posture, put your fingertips on the floor behind your buttocks.
Avoid	Rounding the lower back.
Organ and chakra connection	Balancing on your tailbone is a good grounding exercise (which stimulates the 1st chakra). But be sure you're also lifting up the chest and opening the heart (4th chakra).
Especially good during	PMS, menstruation and menopause—although this is more of a general posture and doesn't offer specific hormonal relief.
Avoid during	Pregnancy. A big belly makes this too hard to balance. Don't risk it.
Transition to the next posture	Rest your elbows on the floor behind your back or place a pillow under your spine.

12. Fish Pose Variations

(B)   Fish Pose Variations   (A)

Pull your elbows behind your body, straighten your legs, lift the chest to the ceiling and shoulders off the floor. Arch your upper back as much as you comfortably can. Don't throw back the head. Keep your neck straight, as if your head were on a shelf, and look up (A). If this is hard on your shoulders, you can do this posture supported on a big, hard floor pillow. Lay your torso over the pillow and extend your arms over your head as you open the chest. Put the soles of the feet together and let the knees fall open (B).

Movement Mandala	For both variations—lift your chest up the vertical as you pull your naval down toward the floor. Keep neck and head horizontal.
Oppositions	For A—pull your navel down and chest up. Reach the head in one direction, the legs and tailbone in the other. For B—chest lifts, navel pulls down, legs open, while tailbone pulls in one direction, arms and head in the other.
Works	Lower and upper back.
Stretches	Chest, shoulders, abdominals.
Variation	If you don't have a flexible lower back, bend your knees slightly in both postures so that your heels touch the floor.
Avoid	Dropping your head back into an unsupported position.
Organ and chakra connection	The emphasis here is on opening your chest and heart (the 4th chakra). However, the arched spine, combined with pulling the tailbone down, also stimulates the adrenal glands (1st chakra).
Especially good during	Menstruation for menstrual cramps. Also good for PMS and menopause. This posture helps rejuvenate tired adrenal glands (which get depleted under stress).
Avoid during	Pregnancy. This back bend position is uncomfortable with a big belly and not advised after the fourth month.
Transition to the next posture	Bend your knees, roll them to the side and sit up.

Bound (A) into Unbound Pose (B)

Sit up straight on your "sit bones" with the spine vertical and hold on to your feet. Your arms should feel strong, almost rigid. This helps open the chest and roll the shoulders back and down. Pull up through the head and let the knees open. Incline your torso slightly forward without rounding the spine (A). To transition into Unbound pose, place your fingertips or palms on the floor behind your buttocks. Lift the hips off the floor and press one hip up and forward. Open the chest (B). Sit your hips back down and repeat on the other side.

Movement Mandala	Bound pose—torso vertical. Unbound pose—torso leans back on an upper diagonal.
Oppositions	Bound pose—head pulls up, tailbone down. Lower back contracts, abdominal muscles pull in and chest lifts. Unbound pose—one hip presses forward and up, while the shoulder on that same side pulls back.
Works	Bound pose—torso stabilizers and shoulders. Unbound pose—shoulders, arms, back.
Stretches	Bound pose—inner thigh and torso. Unbound pose—Hip flexor, inner thigh, torso, shoulder.
Variation	Turn the Unbound pose into a full spiral for the spine. As your left hip presses up and forward, turn your head and shoulders to the left.
Avoid	Collapsing your chest in the Bound pose.

Organ and chakra connection	Bound pose lets you anchor down into your tailbone and align up through your spine to the top of your head. This posture, therefore, can bring awareness to all the chakras. Unbound pose opens the heart (4th chakra) and the slight arch in the back stimulates the sexual and digestive organs (2nd and 3rd chakras).
Especially good during	Bound pose is fine during pregnancy (also menstruation, PMS and menopause). Unbound pose is especially good for relieving menstrual cramps.
Avoid during	Avoid the Unbound pose during pregnancy unless you only hold the posture for about ten seconds and it doesn't bother your shoulders, wrists or hips.
Transition to the next posture	Open the legs to the northeast and northwest corners. Bend the knees and keep the soles of the feet on the floor.

14. Straddle Pose Variations

(B)   Straddle Pose Variations   (A)

These variations on a favorite dancer's stretch solve some of the placement problems associated with that original posture (rounded torso, unsupported abdominal muscles, elevated shoulders). First, open the legs to the northeast and northwest corners, keeping knees bent, feet flat on the floor. Open the legs only as wide as you can and still hold your torso upright. If you're not very flexible, keep your right knee bent and straighten the left leg (if flexible, straighten both legs). Lift the rib cage up and then face your torso to the northwest corner. Slide your torso horizontally to the right until the spine laterally bends over the knee. (Your torso and leg should be in the northeast corner.) Place the right elbow on the right knee or the floor and extend the left arm up the vertical (A). To deepen the stretch, extend the arm over your head on an upper diagonal. Make sure your shoulder stays down and the arm doesn't hang in front of your face (B). Keep the opposite leg reaching out in the other direction. Repeat on the other side.

Movement Mandala	Legs to the northeast and northwest corners. Torso slides to the northeast. Arm starts vertical and ends up on an upper diagonal.
Oppositions	As you slide your torso to one side, reach out through the opposite leg. Keep the left hip down as you lift the left arm up (do the same with the right).
Works	Torso stabilizers.
Stretches	Inner thigh and side of torso.
Variation	To get a greater torso stretch, fold the top "reaching" arm behind your head and point the elbow to the ceiling.
Avoid	Stretching your legs so far apart that you can't hold your torso upright. Avoid slumping the shoulders forward.
Organ and chakra connection	The lateral bend compresses the sexual digestive organs (2nd and 3rd chakras) on one side. Be sure to switch sides.
Especially good during	Menstruation, PMS and menopause.
Avoid during	Pregnancy. This stretch can be difficult to support unless you already have a good base of flexibility and abdominal strength.
Transition to the next posture	Bring the legs together, feet on the floor. Hold under the knees and slowly lower your spine to the floor.

On-Your-Back Postures

Do postures 15, 16 and 17 in succession. Avoid 16 and 17 if they feel too strenuous. Try them again when you're feeling stronger.

15. Bridge Pose Variations

(B)   Bridge Pose Variations   (A)

Lying with knees bent and feet flat on the floor, place legs parallel and hip distance apart. Hold on to your ankles if you can reach them easily. If not, keep your arms by your sides, palms facing down. Begin this move as a pelvic tilt—slightly lift the pubic bone to the ceiling and gradually lift the whole spine off the floor. Squeeze the buttocks to support the spine (A). It feels good to lift and lower the spine a few times before taking this stretch to its extreme. (Remember, when you lift and lower, do so one vertebra at a time.) To lift further, raise the spine again, lift the hips to the highest point and raise the heels. Extend the arms overhead (B). In both Bridge poses, the chest and shoulders lift, while the abdominals pull down and hollow out like a bowl. Keep the back of the neck long. Your weight should be on your shoulder blades—not your neck.

Movement Mandala Lift the hips off the floor until the entire body forms a diagonal line.

Oppositions Lift your chest and hips up. Pull your navel down. Reach your tailbone out away from the navel and the head in the opposite direction.

Works Thighs, back and abdominals.

Stretches	Abdominals, hip flexors, chest and front of shoulder.
Variation	Try folding your arms over your chest when lifted in the Bridge to stretch your upper back.
Avoid	Lifting your hips up *without* using abdominals for support.
Organ and chakra connection	This posture primarily stimulates the adrenal glands (1st chakra).
Especially good during	Menopause and PMS.
Avoid during	Menstruation. This and all inverted postures take the blood flow back into the body. This position is not good during pregnancy either. The weight of the belly is uncomfortable here and can cut off blood flow into the uterus.
Transition to the next posture	Bring your arms by your sides and support your hips in your hands (rest your elbows on the floor), while your hips are raised.

16. Bridge with Leg Lift into Modified Plough

Bridge with Leg Lift (A) into Modified Plough (B)

Getting into these postures takes a bit of finesse. To get into the Bridge with Leg Lift, slide one hand under each hip, one at a time, to support your lower back with your forearms. Lift the right leg up, foot to the ceiling, but keep that knee bent. Let gravity drop the knee toward your chest (A). Hold for at least ten seconds, lower the right foot to the floor, lift the left and hold. To get into position for the Modified Plough, pull one knee to the chest, then the other, so both thighs are parallel to the floor. Rest the weight of your torso in your hands so you feel the stretch in your lower back (not the shoulders). Point the toes to the ceiling (B). Large-breasted women might need to open the legs to get a deep lower back stretch.

Movement Mandala In both postures, feet point up the vertical line. Spine forms a diagonal.

Oppositions Bridge with Leg Lift—keep lifting the chest and hips up as you pull abdominals down. Modified Plough—point feet up as hips drop down into your hands.

Works Bridge with Leg Lift—abdominal and lower back stabilizers. Also the thigh of the supporting leg. Modified Plough—abdominal stabilizers.

Stretches Bridge with Leg Lift—torso, hip flexor and, with leg elevated, buttocks and hamstring. Modified Plough—lower back and buttocks.

Variation If your back and abdominals are strong and you want a good hip flexor stretch while doing the Bridge with Leg Lift, straighten your lifted leg and lower until parallel to the floor. For an even deeper stretch, bend that knee slightly so the foot touches the floor. This is not a beginner's move.

Avoid Both postures if you have very weak abdominal and lower back muscles.

Organ and chakra connection Bridge with Leg Lift—as with a regular Bridge, this stimulates the adrenal glands (1st chakra). Modified Plough—this rounded torso position compresses and rejuvenates both sexual and digestive organs (2nd and 3rd chakras).

Especially good during Menopause and PMS.

Avoid during Menstruation and pregnancy for the reasons listed in the regular Bridge.

Transition to the next posture Return to the Modified Plough.

(B)   Shoulder Stands   (A)

Neither of these shoulder stands will compress the vertebrae in your neck. Rest your hips in the hands as in the Modified Plough. Slowly unfold your legs and lift them on a diagonal line, with feet over your face (A). To do a completely vertical shoulder stand, you should use a firm pillow under your shoulders to let your head hang freely as you point your legs up the vertical. Hold your lower back to stabilize the spine (B). The safest and easiest way to get out of these positions is to return to the Modified Plough position and slowly roll your spine to the floor. End by pulling both knees to the chest (hold *under* the knees to protect delicate knee joints).

Movement Mandala Either legs and torso reach up the vertical line or both form diagonals.

Oppositions In a vertical shoulder stand, pull the feet up. Gravity pulls the shoulders down on their own. Stabilize by holding in abdominal muscles and supporting your lower back with your hands. In a diagonal shoulder stand, pull the hips down toward the floor as you extend the legs. Pull the navel down into the spine.

Works	Abdominal stabilizers and lower back.
Stretches	Shoulders, upper back (and buttocks when legs are on a diagonal).
Variation	If the shoulder stands are too difficult, stick with the Modified Plough or skip them all.
Avoid	Scrunching the vertebrae in your neck. Rest on your shoulders (not your neck).
Organ and chakra connection	In both shoulder stands, the throat is the focal point. Thus, your thyroid is stimulated here (5th chakra). These inverted postures also stimulate the entire endocrine system (all the glands and chakras).
Especially good during	Menopause. Inverted postures help relieve hot flashes and night sweats. They also lower blood pressure and stress—so they're good for PMS, too.
Avoid during	Menstruation, as it disrupts the natural downward flow. During pregnancy it is not advised, as gravity pulls the uterus toward the head. Plus, it's a difficult move.
Transition to the next posture	After rolling your spine to the floor, pull your knees up to your chest and expose the soles of the feet to the ceiling.

18. Welcome Home, Honey

(A)   Welcome Home, Honey   (B)

I can't take credit for the name of this posture. A woman who takes my class heard it from her yoga teacher, who probably heard it from *her* yoga teacher.

And so, "Welcome Home, Honey" (to which I always add, "on a good day"), passes into the yoga lexicon. With knees into your chest, legs parallel and feet flexed toward the ceiling, pull your feet and knees down toward your shoulders. Let the lower back lift slightly off the floor (A). To add an inner thigh stretch, place arms *inside* the legs, open legs wider and gently pull your knees to the floor (B). On this one, you can point or flex the feet.

Movement Mandala	Align your thighs on the horizontal and your shins on the vertical.
Oppositions	Press the knees down to let the lower back lift up; keep the feet up. Reach out through the tailbone and up through the top of the head to elongate the spine. Pull your abdominals down into the floor.
Works	Thighs and abdominal stabilizers.
Stretches	Lower and middle back and inner thighs.
Variation	If pointing the feet up to the ceiling is too hard, simply bend the knees into a tighter angle, folding into a ball.
Avoid	Bouncing your legs. Bouncing is risky and does nothing to increase flexibility. It actually confuses the muscles (they don't know if they should shorten or stretch).
Organ and chakra connection	With the lower back lifted off the floor, the rounded spine compresses and stimulates the adrenal glands and sexual and digestive organs (1st, 2nd and 3rd chakras).
Especially good during	PMS and menopause.
Avoid during	Menstruation—unless you keep the lower back down on the floor. During pregnancy you don't want to be on your back for long, plus it's tempting to take the inner thigh stretch too far.
Transition to the next posture	Pull the knees into your chest and roll them to the east and lie in a fetal position.

Open Hip Stretch (B)   Lower Back Stretch (A)

You'll already be on your side when you start. But to reestablish your bearings, imagine your head is pointed north. Make sure both knees point east, open arms to east and west and turn your head to the west (A). To add the Open Hip Stretch, extend your leg that's on top to the south, so the hip opens and drops back into the floor. Extend the arm on that same side to the north so the arm and leg form a straight line to stretch the side of the body (B). When finished, roll both knees back to center and mirror repeat A and B on the other side.

Movement Mandala   Lower Back Stretch—knees east, arms east and west; look west. Open Hip Stretch—one knee east (or west), one leg south and arm of same side north; arm and leg on same side are straight.

Oppositions   Let the spine twist as you reach in opposite directions with arms and legs.

Works   Abdominal stabilizers and lower back.

Stretches   Lower Back Stretch—lower and upper back, chest. Open Hip Stretch—front and side of hip, chest and shoulder.

Variation	To deepen the Lower Back Stretch, cross the right knee over the left and lower both knees to the left. Repeat on the other side.
Avoid	Shortchanging the stretch. This is a *relaxing* pose.
Organ and chakra connection	Twisting poses stimulate the adrenals and ovaries (1st and 2nd chakras).
Especially good during	Menopause, PMS and menstruation.
Avoid during	The Lower Back Stretch is safe to do when pregnant but you should avoid staying down on your back for more than thirty seconds in the Open Hip Stretch.
Transition to the next posture	Pull both knees to the chest and roll onto your side.

On-Your-Side Postures

Do postures 20 and 21 in succession on one side before repeating on other side.

20. Lord Vishnu's Couch Variations

(B)   Lord Vishnu's Couch Variations   (A)

Lie on your left side. Reorient yourself so you *face* north, although your head should point west and your feet to the east (keep your body in a straight line). Bend your bottom knee for balance (it'll point to the northeast). (You can support your head on your hand or rest it on the shoulder.) Pull the right knee up to your right shoulder, with the elbow inside the crook of your knee. The shin aligns up the vertical axis (A). To deepen the stretch and add the hamstrings, hold the inner thigh, calf, foot or big toe and straighten the right leg (B). (You don't have to straighten it all the way to stretch the hamstring.) In both postures, the hips should be stacked directly on top of each other, on the vertical axis to prevent you from rolling backward. Use abdominal strength to hold yourself up.

Movement Mandala	Stretching the right leg, head points west, bottom knee bends to the northeast, foot points east. Point the foot up the vertical with knee bent or straight.
Oppositions	For A—press the heel and knee down. For B—press the heel up. For both—hold in the abdominals for support and lengthen the waistline as it touches the floor. In other words, the hip and shoulder making contact with the floor should pull in opposite horizontal directions.
Works	Abdominal and lower back stabilizers.
Stretches	Inner thigh and hamstring.
Variation	If you have difficulty holding yourself up, do this with your back against a wall. If you want to challenge yourself (and build torso-stabilizing strength), straighten your supporting leg on the floor, so your body forms a straight line from head to toe.
Avoid	Dropping your top shoulder or hip to the back. Balance on your side throughout.
Organ and chakra connection	This posture doesn't directly stimulate any particular organ or chakra; however, to maintain your balance, focus your attention on the solar plexus (3rd chakra).
Especially good during	Menopause, PMS and menstruation. This is more of a general exercise, however, and not a woman-specific posture.
Avoid during	Pregnancy, if your belly is so large that you can't hold yourself up on the side. However, if that's not a problem, this exercise causes no harm and is especially good when you lie on your side.
Transition to the next posture	If your bottom leg is straight, bend it. Let go of the foot and lower the leg.

Rest the head on your shoulder and lower the arm and leg to the horizontal. Make sure the leg is parallel, not turned out at the hip. Place the extended foot on the floor *behind* the supporting leg (move the supporting leg forward if you have to). Otherwise you won't get the hip stretch. Hold the wrist of the top arm and gently pull it overhead.

Movement Mandala If you could see yourself from the ceiling, you should see the top arm and leg extended in a perfect straight line, from west to east. From the front, however, your extended leg *won't* form a perfect horizontal. Let the leg drop below the horizontal line.

Oppositions Reach the arm and leg away from each other.

Works Abdominal and lower back stabilizers.

Stretches Outer hip, obliques, lats and shoulder.

Avoid Resting your top leg on your bottom leg. Make sure it falls behind the other leg.

Organ and chakra connection As in the previous exercise, the solar plexus is your point of focus (the 3rd chakra) although this posture doesn't directly stimulate any particular glands.

Especially good during Menopause, PMS and menstruation. This is more of a general exercise, however, and not a woman-specific posture.

Avoid during Pregnancy, if your belly is so large that you can't hold yourself up on the side. However, if that's not a problem, this exercise causes no harm and is especially good when you lie on your left side.

Transition to the next posture After you repeat these two postures on the other side, pull both knees to your chest and sit up. Keep both knees over to the left.

Do postures 22 and 23 on one side before switching legs.

22. Dancer's Stretch Variations

(B)   Dancer's Stretch Variations   (A)

Sit on your right hip with both knees to the right. Lift onto your right elbow and right knee. Extend the left leg straight so the foot rests on the floor. Lift the left arm first up the vertical (A) then overhead to an upper diagonal. For a deeper stretch along the side of your torso, rest your weight on your *hand* instead of your elbow. Keep your shoulder down as you extend the arm on first a vertical, then a diagonal (B). On both versions, the supporting arm should be vertical and the hips should be above (not behind) the knee. Make sure the angle of that supporting knee is 90 degrees.

Movement Mandala   The supporting arm should be vertical. The extended leg forms a lower diagonal. The extended arm begins vertical and progresses to an upper diagonal.

Oppositions   When the top arm is vertical, reach up through the fingertips and down through the supporting knee. When the top arm reaches up the upper diagonal, reach the extended leg in the opposite direction.

Works	Thigh, upper arm, torso stabilizers.
Stretches	Hip, abdominals, chest and shoulders.
Variation	You can do this exercise on both knees *without* extending one leg. This stretches the hip and side of the torso.
Avoid	Bending your bottom knee into more than a 90-degree angle. Your hips should be lifted as high as possible off the floor (don't sit down near or on your foot).
Organ and chakra connection	This stretch opens the chest and heart (4th chakra) and stimulates the thymus gland.
Especially good during	Menstruation, PMS and menopause.
Avoid during	Pregnancy, if you have trouble with the balance. Otherwise, it shouldn't cause problems.
Translation to the next posture	Return the arm to vertical, then bend the knees and sit on the floor. Repeat on the other side. After you finish the second side, remain seated with both legs to one side.

23. Modified Splits

(B)   Modified Splits   (A)

Once again get your bearings. Face north. After completing the Dancer's Stretch with the first leg, once again sit on your right hip, with both knees to the right, both legs in a **Z** shape (knees form 90-degree angles). Keep the front foot approximately twelve inches in front of your pubic bone. Balancing on your right hip, turn your torso to the northeast. Place fingertips on the floor and incline your torso gently forward, keeping the back *straight* (A). To deepen the buttocks stretch, slowly walk the fingers forward, round the back over the leg and rest elbows on the floor (B).

Movement Mandala	Sitting on right hip—right knee to northeast, left knee to northwest or west. Torso to the northeast.
Oppositions	Pull the hips back slightly as you incline the chest forward with a flat back. Pull the hips back more as the back rounds forward.
Works	Torso stabilizers.
Stretches	Hip flexor of back leg, buttocks on the front leg. Lower back when rounded.
Variation	If you want a deeper hip flexor stretch, straighten the back leg more.
Avoid	Placing the front foot too close to the body (it stresses the knee and diminishes the buttocks stretch).
Organ and chakra connection	This forward bend position puts gentle pressure on the ovaries, uterus and digestive organs (the 2nd and 3rd chakras).
Especially good during	Menopause, PMS and menstruation (good for cramps). When you roll up out of the rounded posture, the release of pressure sends a rush of freshly oxygenated blood into these areas.
Avoid during	Pregnancy. The belly gets in the way when the back is rounded. However, you can do version A with relative ease.
Transition to the next posture	Move both knees to the left and repeat on the other side. When finished with both sides, take the legs behind you and press up onto hands and knees.

All Fours

Do postures 24, 25 and 26 in succession before repeating the series.

24. Cow and Cat

(A) Cow and Cat (B)

The lower back initiates all the movement in this posture. Inhale, lower the tailbone to the floor to round the back (the Cow—A). Use your abdominal and back muscles to control this slow motion. Exhale, lift the tailbone to the ceiling and arch the lower back (the Cat—B). You can bend elbows slightly.

Movement Mandala   Cow—drop the tailbone and head down the vertical to round the back. Cat—lift the tailbone and head up the vertical to arch the back.

Oppositions   Cow—as the lower back rounds, the navel pulls up and the head and tailbone pull down. Cat—as lower back arches, the shoulders and hips pull up (avoid the temptation to lose your support in the abdominal muscles).

Works   Abdominals and back muscles, chest, shoulders, arms.

Stretches   Lower back, abdominals, chest, upper back.

Variation   Rest on your elbows if your wrists hurt.

Avoid   Throwing your neck back or moving the spine without controlling the torso muscles.

Organ and Chakra Connection	Because the spine rounds and arches around the solar plexus, this posture mostly stimulates the sexual and digestive organs (2nd and 3rd chakras).
Especially good during	Pregnancy. Gravity increases blood flow into the uterus and offers back relief. Also fine for menopause, menstruation and PMS.
Avoid during	Not applicable. This is a very gentle exercise.
Transition to the next posture	Return to a "flat" back position. Avoid the Upward Dog if pregnant, especially with a very big belly. Move right onto the Downward-facing Plank pose or Downward Dog.

25. *Upward Dog into Downward-facing Plank Pose*

Upward Dog (A) into Downward-facing Plank Pose (B)

Upward Dog—balance on your arms and the front of your thighs (or tops of your feet) and lift your hips off the floor to protect your lower back. Keep legs hip-distance apart or closer (closer is harder because it narrows your base of support). Hands should be directly under your shoulders, arms vertical. Press the shoulders down into your back (don't shrug) as if pressing your shoulder blades into your back pockets. Lift the chest and head up (A). To move into the Downward-facing Plank pose, bend the toes back. Press on to the balls of your feet and lift the torso and legs off the floor, as if preparing to do a push-up. Don't drop or raise the hips. Keep the body in a continuous diagonal line, from shoulders to heels. Flatten and widen the upper back. To make this move more challenging, lift one leg off the floor, hold, then switch legs (this makes the chest and shoulders work harder).

Movement Mandala	Upward Dog—head and arms vertical, legs horizontal. Downward-facing Plank pose—diagonal line from heels to the top of your head.
Oppositions	Upward Dog—lift the head and chest up, pubic bone and shoulders down. Squeeze buttocks and pull in the navel. Downward-facing Plank pose—press in opposite directions through the heels and head. Pull the navel up into your spine and squeeze the buttocks. Widen your shoulder blades to avoid shrugging the upper back.
Works	Upward Dog—lower and upper back, shoulders, arms. Downward-facing Plank pose—chest, arms and some thigh.
Stretches	Upward Dog—chest, hip flexors, thighs. Downward-facing Plank pose—upper back, some hamstring.
Variation	For a different transition from the Cow and Cat, lower your chest to the floor in the Cat Stretch. Then slide your chin, chest and hips along the floor (I call it a "shoot-through"). Place hands under your shoulders and lift into Upward Dog.
Avoid	Dangerously arching your back in the Upward Dog. Don't sag your hips toward the floor in the Downward-facing Plank pose.
Organ and chakra connection	Upward Dog—stimulates ovaries, digestive system and adrenals (1st, 2nd and 3rd chakras). Downward-facing Plank pose—more of a full-body strength move, less specific chakra and organ stimulation.
Especially good during	Upward Dog is especially good for menopause, menstruation and PMS. All arched-back poses stimulate the adrenals, which run low during these times. The Downward-facing Plank pose is a good strengthener during menopause, menstruation and PMS. It develops upper body strength and is easier to do than push-ups.
Avoid during	Pregnancy. The Upward Dog is not advised. However, the Downward-facing Plank pose is safe during pregnancy if you have a base of upper body strength to support it.
Transition to the next posture	Bend your knees and press your buttocks up to the ceiling.

(A)   **Downward Dog Variations**   (B)

Bend your knees *before* you press your buttocks to the ceiling. The most important part of this posture is lengthening the spine. Walk your hands back until your arms and back are straight. Keep the knees bent and lift the heels (A). If balancing on your hands bothers wrists or shoulders, stay on your elbows (B). In both versions, lift your tailbone up the vertical. The lower back should feel slightly *arched*, not *rounded*. Knees stay bent and heels lifted.

Movement Mandala	Press your tailbone up to vertical. Arms, legs and torso form diagonals.
Oppositions	Push away with the hands or elbows so the back is supported and straight. Although the heels stay lifted, pull them down (to feel grounded in your feet). Lift the tailbone up and pull the sit bones back away from the heels.
Works	Arms, lower back and thighs.
Stretches	Shoulders, torso, hips, hamstrings.
Variation	If you're very flexible, lower one heel to the ground and straighten one leg. Switch legs before you try it with both legs straight. Never force the heels down. If pregnant or menstruating, try a Downward Dog with the torso horizontal. Hold onto a ballet barre or something you can't pull over as you sit your hips away from your arms. Keep the knees bent and legs wide enough to maintain balance.
Avoid	Rounding your spine. This can irritate spinal ligaments.

Organ and chakra connection	This bent-over posture stimulates adrenals and sexual and digestive organs (1st, 2nd and 3rd chakras).
Especially good during	Menopause and PMS. All inverted postures have a positive effect on all glands that control hormone production. They also lower blood pressure and leave you energized.
Avoid during	Menstruation. Avoid all inversions at this time. Avoid when pregnant, as well. Do the horizontal variation listed above.
Transition to the next posture	Come down to your knees to repeat the series. When finished, lie facedown on the floor (unless you're pregnant).

27. Half Locust into Full Bow

Half Locust (A) into Full Bow (B)

Lying facedown (with forehead on the floor and back of the neck long) put your hands under your hip bones so they don't dig into the floor. Lift one leg, but not the hip, off the floor (A). If this feels moderately easy, raise both shoulders slightly at the same time but don't arch the back. (Pull shoulder blades down onto your spine.) Alternate legs. To get into the Full Bow pose, hold both ankles, press the feet back into your hands, and raise the legs and shoulders off the floor (B). Although this is a full arched position, maintain control of the abdominal muscles.

Movement Mandala	The Half Locust begins in a horizontal. Raise one leg toward an upper diagonal. The Full Bow lifts arms and lower legs toward upper diagonals.

Oppositions	Half Locust—lift the leg (and optional shoulders) up while you pull the navel down. Full Bow—press the ankles back into the hands and chest forward. Pull the navel up even though the belly presses down.
Works	Half Locust and Full Bow—lower and upper back, buttocks.
Stretches	Half Locust and Full Bow—hip flexors, chest, shoulders, abdominals.
Variation	If you can do a Half Locust with ease, try lifting both legs and shoulders at the same time. If you can't do the Full Bow, try a Half Bow. Hold and lift one leg at a time.
Avoid	Thrusting your legs up without controlling the torso muscles.
Organ and chakra connection	This position stimulates ovaries and digestive organs (2nd and 3rd chakras).
Especially good during	Menopause, PMS and menstruation. Eases cramps, erratic bleeding and hot flashes.
Avoid during	Pregnancy. Don't squish that baby!
Transition to the next posture	Press up onto hands and knees.

28. Thigh Incline into Half Back Bend

Come onto your knees (put some sort of padding, like a rolled-up towel, under your knees if this bothers your knees). Feet are relaxed (don't flex the toes). Incline your torso back in a diagonal line from shoulders to knees (A). Hold for as long as comfortable. Return the torso to vertical. To get into the Half Back Bend, circle one arm over head (from front to back) and rest it behind you on your ankle. For an oppositional stretch, lift the other arm up to the ceiling (B). Keep the chest lifting in both postures and the neck in line with your spine (don't throw back the head). To get out of the Half Back Bend, imagine you're holding a gymnast's ring in the hand of your vertical arm. Slowly pull yourself up to vertical.

Movement Mandala	Thigh Incline—body forms a diagonal from shoulders to knees. Half Back Bend—both the supporting and lifted arms form vertical lines.
Oppositions	Thigh Incline—as body leans back, keep lifting the chest and abdominals forward. Half Back Bend—as torso arcs back, press the chest up. As you press down into the arm behind you, reach up the other arm.
Works	Thigh Incline—thighs, lower back and abdominals. Half Back Bend—lower back.

Thigh Incline (A) into Half Back Bend (B)

Stretches Thigh Incline—abdominals, thighs and hip flexors. Half Back Bend—chest, abdominals and shoulder.

Variation If the Half Back Bend is still too challenging, press your fists into your middle back (at your kidneys) and lift the chest up. Only slightly arch the lower back.

Avoid Getting into either of these positions too quickly or without controlling the torso muscles.

Organ and chakra connection Thigh Incline—mostly accentuates the heart (4th chakra), also the thymus gland. Half Back Bend—stimulates the adrenals, sexual and digestive organs, heart and thymus gland (the 1st, 2nd, 3rd and 4th chakras).

Especially good during Menopause, menstruation and PMS. Both are good revitalizing postures.

Avoid during Pregnancy. Both postures can be hard to control with a large pregnant belly.

Transition to the next posture Return to hands and knees.

(A)   Child's Pose Variations   (B)

Before you sit back on your heels, extend your arms as far forward as possible. Slowly sit back, almost resisting dragging your hands across the floor (A). Hold this posture for at least ten seconds to stretch the upper back. For a deeper lower back stretch, place the arms by your sides. Rest your forehead on the floor (B).

Movement Mandala Sit back on your feet and drag arms slowly on a horizontal line.

Oppositions Resist pulling the arms along the floor as you sit the hips back (A). With arms by your sides, let your forehead and tailbone hang down to the floor as your abdominal muscles pull up into the spine.

Works This is a resting pose. However, hold in the abdominals.

Stretches Your whole spine, buttocks, shoulders and neck.

Variation For an inner thigh stretch, widen legs about eight inches before you sit back. To stretch one side of the back, sit both hips to one side of both ankles. Switch sides.

Avoid Shortchanging your stretch. Stay here for a while to feel the layers of tension peel away.

Organ and chakra connection This posture relieves discomfort in the ovaries and stomach, so it's mostly a 2nd and 3rd chakra posture. However, because the forehead rests on the floor, it also rejuvenates the 6th and 7th chakras—and can also be good for clearing the mind and relieving a headache.

Especially good during Menstruation (great for relieving cramps and low backache), PMS and menopause. This forward bend position not only rejuvenates sexual and digestive organs, it also calms the mind and nervous system.

Avoid during Pregnancy, if your belly is large. You won't be able to do this.

Transition to the next posture Come back to hands and knees.

(B)   Pretzel Pose Variations   (A)

I like this stretch better than a seated twist because gravity assists the stretch—so you get more twist for less effort. From hands and knees; slide your left arm across the floor, so it passes under your chest and behind the right hand. Slowly lower yourself down onto your left shoulder and the left side of your head. Rest your right hand on the small of your back, with the palm down. Look up the vertical axis (A). To make this a balance exercise plus hamstring stretch, extend your right leg back to the southeast. Balance on the ball of the right foot and press the right heel back (B). To switch sides, put your right hand on the floor, bend your extended leg and push up to hands and knees.

Movement Mandala	With head north, slide your left arm to the east and rest on the left shoulder. To add the leg, extend the left leg to the southeast. Repeat on the other side in the opposite directions.
Oppositions	With the left shoulder down, pull the right shoulder back.
Works	Lower back, abdominals, hip and shoulder stabilizers.
Stretches	Chest, shoulders, upper back, lower back, abdominals and buttocks of the extended leg.
Variation	This is the variation of a seated twist.
Avoid	Twisting your neck too much in this position. Let your head rest comfortably on the floor.
Organ and chakra connection	Twists stimulate the adrenal glands, ovaries and digestive organs (1st, 2nd and 3rd chakras).
Especially good during	Menopause, PMS, menstruation and pregnancy.

Avoid during	Pregnancy if it bothers you in any way. Otherwise, it's safe.
Transition to the next posture	After finishing the stretch on the second side, return to hands and knees, press the balls of the feet on the floor and walk hands back toward your feet until your heels touch down. Spread legs hip-distance apart for greater balance. Keep knees bent.

31. Deep Squat Variations

(A)   Deep Squat Variations   (B)

These squats might look a little intimidating but, done properly, they're safe and most people can at least do version A without hurting the back or knees. Toilets and chairs have done away with the need for doing deep squats in modern culture. But this natural position is good for sexual and digestive organs, also elimination and childbirth. Begin with spine parallel to the floor, feet slightly wider apart than hips. Place your fingertips on the floor just inside or behind the heels. This lets you rest your thighs on your elbows. Use the arms to hold the legs open (A). To deepen the squat, keep both heels on the floor and ease your buttocks down below your knees. Press the legs open with your elbows (B). Keep your weight back in your heels (if this is still too hard on knees or back, skip it or try the variation below).

Movement Mandala	For A—maintain a horizontal spine or the tailbone can lower slightly below horizontal. B—lower hips so the tailbone points down the vertical.
Oppositions	Press your knees open with your elbows in both versions of this squat and keep the weight in your heels and lower back as the head pulls forward.
Works	Thighs and abdominals.

Stretches	Lower back and buttocks.
Variation	Try version B while pushing your lower back against a wall.
Avoid	Bouncing into the deep squat. Go slowly to protect your knees and test your balance.
Organ and chakra connection	This stimulates adrenals and sexual and digestive organs (1st, 2nd and 3rd chakras).
Especially good during	PMS, menstruation, menopause and pregnancy—if it doesn't bother you.
Avoid during	Times of extreme fatigue or knee injury.
Transition to the next posture	Place your hands on your knees and return your spine to the horizontal. Put your hands on the floor.

32. Runner's Stretch Variations

(B)   Runner's Stretch Variations   (A)

Slide your right leg straight behind you. Place the ball of this foot on the floor and press the heel back. Make sure your front (left) heel stays on the floor and front knee remains over or behind the ankle. (Don't let the knee hang out beyond the toe.) To stretch your inner thigh, slide your left elbow under your left knee (A). For more of a torso stretch, place your left hand on the floor next to the instep of the right foot. Extend your right arm up the vertical (B). In both variations, you'll get a deeper stretch, if after setting the arm position, you raise the hips slightly and then lower them, settling gently into the stretch.

Movement Mandala	For A—set your body in a straight but slightly diagonal line from heel to head; you'll be on a slight angle above the horizontal. For B—keep the same body position as above, but align both arms and look up the vertical.
Oppositions	For A—the head pulls forward as the heels pull back. For B—pull the hips and supporting shoulder down as the extended arm lifts up.
Works	Thigh, abdominals, upper back.
Stretches	Lower back, inner thigh, hip flexor, calf. Chest and shoulder also stretch on version B.
Variation	If either of these arm postures is too difficult, place both hands on either side of the knee. Bend your back leg to make this easier.
Avoid	Rounding your upper back during any version of this stretch. Keep the spine long. If your front heel lifts off the floor, walk your back foot farther behind you and slide your hips back.
Organ and chakra connection	Both postures stimulate the adrenals and sexual and digestive organs (1st, 2nd and 3rd chakras).
Especially good during	Menopause, PMS and pregnancy if you have the strength and flexibility to do this.
Avoid during	Menstruation and pregnancy if feeling weak. Otherwise, this posture is fine if you're strong enough to do it.
Transition to the next posture	After repeating on both sides, press both legs back (as if in a Downward-facing Plank pose), bend the knees, lift the buttocks in the air (as if in Downward Dog) and gradually walk your hands to your feet. Place the heels down.

Upper Body (A) Cascade into Semisquat (B) and Roll-up

Roll your weight back into your *heels* for this final stretch and completion move. Bend your knees so that your chest rests on your thighs. This supports your lower back (but draw in your abdominals for extra support). Lace your fingertips together, put your hands behind your head and let the head hang freely (A). To transition into the next posture, place your hands on your thighs and flatten your spine so it's parallel to the floor. With weight still back in your heels and hips, raise your torso into a Semisquat position, with spine on an upper diagonal. From here, you have the option to rise up to standing (as if coming out of a squat) or rounding the vertebrae to vertical, one at a time.

Movement Mandala   Let your knees bend so much on the Upper Body Cascade that your thighs and spine form diagonals. In the Semisquat position, your spine forms an upper diagonal.

Oppositions   On the Upper Body Cascade, your head and tailbone act like two counterweights. Both drop down while the navel pulls up to the vertical. On the Semisquat, pull back into the tailbone and heels and reach forward through the top of the head.

Works   Upper Body Cascade—abdominal stabilizers and thighs. Semisquat—lower back and thighs.

Stretches	Upper Body Cascade—upper and lower back and buttocks. Semisquat—abdominals, buttocks and hips.
Variation	Before doing these final postures, you might want to lie on your back (in "Dead Man's pose") with legs straight, arms by your sides and eyes closed. Or sit in a meditative posture and simply enjoy the stillness and sensations in your body.
Avoid	Using straight legs on either of these final postures.
Organ and chakra connection	Upper Body Cascade—stimulates adrenals and sexual and digestive organs (1st, 2nd and 3rd chakras). As you return to a vertical posture, realign your torso and put attention on all chakras.
Especially good during	Menstruation, PMS, menopause and pregnancy. In all situations, this is a safe move and a very safe way to roll up.
Avoid during	Illness. If you have head congestion, don't stay in the Upper Body Cascade for long.
Transition	Take a moment to "regroup" in this posture before you rush off to whatever you're doing next.

Routine for PMS

Hold each posture for ten to thirty seconds. Do each single posture, pair or series one to four times. You don't have to repeat this entire routine every time. Feel free to choose the postures that work for you according to how you're feeling each day.

Standing Postures (Parallel)

Quad Stretch with Pole

Inclined Pulling Bow Pose

Sit-Back Stretch

Balance Pose

Standing Postures (Turned Out)

The Knee Hold

Karate Pose

Side Balance Pose

Seated Postures

Staff Pose into Back Stretch

Upward-facing Plank Pose

The Half Lotus Sit into the Buttocks Stretch

The Boat

The Fish

Bound into Unbound Pose

Straddle Pose

On-Your-Back Postures

Bridge Pose

Bridge with Leg Lift and Modified Plough

Modified Shoulder Stands

Welcome Home, Honey

Lower Back into Open Hip Stretch

On-Your-Side Postures

Lord Vishnu's Couch

Side Hip Stretch

Dancer's Stretch

Modified Splits

All Fours

Cow and Cat

Upward Dog into Downward-facing Plank Pose

Downward Dog

Half Locust into Full Bow

Thigh Incline into Half Back Bend

Child's Pose

Pretzel Pose

Deep Squats

Runner's Stretch

Upper Body Cascade into Semisquat and Roll-up

Routine for Menstruation

Hold each posture for ten to thirty seconds. Do each single posture, pair or series one to four times. You don't have to repeat this entire routine every time. Feel free to choose the postures that work for you according to how you're feeling each day.

Standing Postures (Parallel)

Sit-Back Stretch

Seated Postures

Staff Pose into Back Stretch

Upward-facing Plank Pose

The Half Lotus Sit into the Buttocks Stretch

The Boat

The Fish

Bound into Unbound Pose

Straddle Pose

On-Your-Back Postures

Lower Back into Open Hip Stretch

On-Your-Side Postures

Lord Vishnu's Couch

Side Hip Stretch

Dancer's Stretch

Modified Splits

All Fours

Cow and Cat

Upward Dog into Downward-facing Plank Pose

Downward Dog variation (hold onto ballet barre, keep spine horizontal)

Half Locust into Full Bow

Thigh Incline into Half Back Bend

Child's Pose

Pretzel Pose

Deep Squats

Runner's Stretch (with caution)

Upper Body Cascade into Semisquat and Roll-up

Routine for Pregnancy

Hold each posture for ten to thirty seconds. Do each single posture, pair or series one to four times. You don't have to repeat this entire routine every time. Feel free to choose the postures that work for you according to how you're feeling each day.

Standing Postures (Parallel)

Sit-Back Stretch

Seated Postures

Bound Pose (but not Unbound)

On-Your-Back Postures

Lower Back into Open Hip Stretch

On-Your-Side Postures

Lord Vishnu's Couch (with precautions)

Side Hip Stretch (with precautions)

Dancer's Stretch (without extending the leg)

Modified Splits (with straight back)

All Fours

Cow and Cat

Downward-facing Plank Pose

Downward Dog variation (hold onto ballet barre, keep spine horizontal)

Pretzel Pose

Deep Squats

Runner's Stretch (with caution)

Upper Body Cascade into Semisquat and Roll-up

Routine for Menopause

Hold each posture for ten to thirty seconds. Do each single posture, pair or series one to four times. You don't have to repeat this entire routine every time. Feel free to choose the postures that work for you according to how you're feeling each day.

Standing Postures (Parallel)

Quad Stretch with Pole

Inclined Pulling Bow Pose

Sit-Back Stretch

Balance Pose

Standing Postures (Turned Out)

The Knee Hold

Karate Pose

Side Balance Pose

Seated Postures

Staff Pose into Back Stretch

Upward-facing Plank Pose

The Half Lotus Sit into the Buttocks Stretch

The Boat

The Fish

Bound into Unbound Pose

Straddle Pose

On-Your-Back Postures

Bridge Pose

Bridge with Leg Lift and Modified Plough

Modified Shoulder Stands

Welcome Home, Honey

Lower Back into Open Hip Stretch

On-Your-Side Postures

Lord Vishnu's Couch

Side Hip Stretch

Dancer's Stretch

Modified Splits

All Fours

Cow and Cat

Upward Dog into Downward-facing Plank Pose

Downward Dog

Half Locust into Full Bow

Thigh Incline into Half Back Bend

Child's Pose

Pretzel Pose

Deep Squats

Runner's Stretch

Upper Body Cascade into Semisquat and Roll-Up

Wrap-Up

If you're starting to wonder when to do all this yoga and fit it in with the other activities your body needs, please see the next chapter for playful suggestions on how to mix, match and balance the many sides of your movement practice.

7   Workouts and Improvisations

People often ask, "How many times each week should I do yoga, aerobics and strength train?" There's really no single formula that works for everyone. We all have different schedules, levels of experience, personalities, desires and all want different things from our physical practice. That's not to say there aren't standard answers to this question. The American College of Sports Medicine and other powers that be agree that in order to achieve optimum health, most people *should* do all of these:

- two to three strength workouts per week

- three to four aerobic workouts per week

- two stretching workouts per week

But the reality is, most people don't have the time or inclination to do all that. This formula doesn't really explain that there are creative ways to blend these activities, still have time for your life and, perhaps most importantly, *enjoy the process!* (Exercise formulas tend to sound like medical prescriptions . . . not too sexy.) Before you can come up with your own formula, you need to determine how much time you can realistically devote each week to exercise, what you like enough to actually *do* and what activities you're *already* doing.

- If you're not exercising at all, then you can start with a clean slate. (Many newcomers to exercise like to start with something easy, like walking two to three days a week or gentle dancing and then slowly add strength exercises and stretching—either on the same day or different days.)

- If you're already exercising regularly, what *type* of workouts do you do the most? (Many women, for instance, favor aerobics and stretch but don't get much if any strength work. They're also a bit reluctant at times to substitute one "fat-burning" aerobic session per week for one strength workout, for fear of gaining weight. But the reality is that strengthening the muscles even just once a week will do more to burn fat and speed the metabolism than excessive amounts of aerobics. Sometimes the hardest thing to change is our beliefs.) Figure out the missing pieces in your program.

- Now that you know what's missing, do you need to learn how to do strength training or yoga postures properly? Do you have access to good teachers or trainers who can meet your budget and schedule? (Hiring a good trainer for at least a few sessions of strength training is well worth the investment. You don't want to waste your time learning bad form and useless exercises. You'll only get frustrated and won't achieve results.)

- What's the ideal number of days each week that your *body* craves for physical activity? This might continue to change as you get in better shape. But remember, everyone needs rest! (If you train religiously with weights, for instance, your body will appreciate at least two solid weeks off each year!)

- Do you know your exercise *personality?* Do you need the support of a group? A trainer? Do you prefer to work out alone? Or do you like a combination?

- Do you thrive on a regular schedule (e.g., weights on Monday, cardio on Tuesday, etc.) or are you more of an "exercise intuitive" and prefer to move your body according to how it feels each day?

Once you know your preferences and habits, then you can make more informed choices about how to balance your regimen with the pieces it might have been missing. Balancing your fitness choices may not make sense to you yet if you're in your twenties or early thirties. At this age, you can get away with following a lopsided program. But when your body turns forty, it's much less forgiving. Knee, shoulder, hip and back injuries, which may have been slowly and silently gathering over time, tend to flare up without apparent warning—and when that happens, sometimes you can't do *any* exercise. Combining strength, flexibility and cardiovascular training won't prevent you from avoiding all injuries or health problems in the future. But if you *don't* do these things, your risks will certainly increase.

As for how to put it all together, there's really no end to the creative ways you can mix and match your exercise activities. Here are two typical scenarios:

- If you belong to a gym but get so busy with work you can only go once a week, you might strength train for twenty-five minutes, do aerobics for twenty-five minutes and yoga stretches for ten. You can also do your aerobics first if you prefer it that way—then strength train and stretch. On the other days, try getting in thirty minutes of walking, stretching or strength training with a band and pole at home.

- If you like to devote an hour a day to formal exercise, five or six days a week, you might do one or two strength workouts a week, take two or three dance or aerobics classes that include strengthening and stretching, and devote one or two more hours to yoga.

One formula won't work for all people—and probably won't continue to work with you either (just when you set your schedule, God tends to make other plans). An exercise practice, like a relationship, is a constantly changing thing. It evolves as you do. If you start to feel stuck in it, bored or to dread your workouts, this is a *big sign* that it's time to refresh your approach, try something new or pick up something you *used* to do but don't do anymore. (Can't remember? Big hint—it's something you love or long to do).

What Makes Your Heart Beat Faster?

I haven't thoroughly addressed the aerobic side of fitness in this book on balance—and it wouldn't be balanced unless I did. Unless you've been living in a cave for the past twenty years, you know that aerobic exercise is nonstop rhythmic motion (such as biking, skating, swimming, rowing, dancing) that keeps your heart healthy and burns excess body fat. When it comes to choosing a form of cardiovascular exercise, I'm a firm believer in applying Joseph Campbell's famous phrase, "Follow your bliss." If running outside in the fresh air, doing laps at your local pool or going out salsa-dancing make your soul sing and your heart beat faster, do it! (And if for some reason, such as injury or time constraint, you can't do it, at least find a substitute sexy enough to hold your attention.)

I follow my cardio bliss with dance. (My second book, *A Woman's Book of Power*, is about creating fun, feminine, flowing dance moves, based on the four universal shapes found in feminine sacred dance styles throughout history—the circle, the spiral, the figure 8 and the snake.) Dance *can* be legitimate aerobic exercise, especially when you do it for forty-five to sixty minutes (with warm-up and cool-down) and at a moderate intensity. A moderate pace is one most people enjoy and it's an honest "fat-burning experience"—especially between the forty-five- and sixty-minute marks. In my experience, dancing to music for an hour goes by much faster than a half hour on a treadmill. When you ride on the music and put your passions into the movements, you forget you're working out! Dancing can also do wonders for your mental health.

Dance from Your Heart

Dance speaks the language of the human heart. You don't have to be a trained dancer to express yourself this way or experience its profound healing power. Dance can be good medicine whether you're just bopping around a dance floor having fun or creating a ritualized story with your movements. Pure spontaneous dance provides whimsy in the face of deadly, creeping seriousness, while more ritualized, conscious movements that tell stories and express emotions provide a profound experience for a dancer and an audience.

I like to improvise to cultivate both types of dance. Improvisations inspire spontaneity and engage your imagination. Next time you're dancing in a place where you feel safe enough to express yourself completely, let yourself dance the passions that dwell in your heart. Try to tell a story with your movements. Interpret the feeling behind the music so clearly that if you had an audience, they'd be able to see and feel what you're trying to say. Here are some easy improvisational story lines to get you started:

- *Dance your higher self.* Be that gracious, beautiful, patient goddess you are when there's nothing that keeps you from knowing it. Inhabit her shimmering presence. Notice her every gesture. Walk in her stature and beauty. Become her. Worship her and be the one who is worshiped! (Enjoy it while you can!)

- *Dance your dark side.* Uncensor yourself. Dance your anger, pettiness, jealousy, and weakness. Confront the dark places that you usually hide from others and yourself. Be bitchy, raunchy, rude, vicious or whatever else you can't be in polite company. Give yourself permission to reveal your shadow. Vent it now.

- *Do a duet between the dark and the light.* You may have already noticed, from the first two improvisations, that the shadow and light have a way of joining forces and getting all mixed up. (For instance, where do you find your sexuality—in the light, in the dark or both?) In the duet, let these two extremes dance in opposition or together.

- *Dance your emotions.* Choose one emotion and follow it through its full course or take your inspiration from watching a baby's face change emotions from moment to moment. Explore the physical sensations associated with different emotions. How do the different emotions—fear, anger, sadness, joy, calm, relief, and so on—affect the *texture* of your movements or the angles or curves of your body? Where are these feelings lodged in your body?

- *Dance your love life.* Imagine a rogues' gallery of perhaps the one, perhaps the three or more major people you've ever fallen in love with, been obsessed with, burned by, rejected, chased, whatever. You know the plot line. Dance with these invisible partners from your past, present and future and tell the story of your heart. Don't be afraid to ham it up and go for the pathos and high drama. This is very cathartic. Notice, at the end, who's still in your life (you!) and who's disappeared. At the end of the dance, you may find yourself laughing or crying or both.

- *Dance your girlhood, your maidenhood, your "motherhood" (even if you're not a mother—dance your "mother spirit") and your wise womanhood.* Inhabit these separate phases in your life or switch back and forth between them. Notice what traits the maiden shares or doesn't share with the mother and wise woman.

- *Dance your ancestry.* Dance your authentic ancestry, the culture of your parents and grandparents, and perhaps dance *their* lives. Or go further back, beyond the family tree that you know, to that place where blood-lines blur and history has been lost. Find an ancestry that stirs you, whether it's real, imagined or perhaps true but so watered down that it's been all but forgotten. Bring it back to life.

- *Dance your gratitude.* Create a devotional dance to express your grate-fulness for being alive. Or create a ritual dance of thanks to someone close to you, living or dead. (If the person is living, ask yourself if you'd ever perform this dance for him or her. Imagine how the person would feel watching you.

- *Dance your daily activities.* Dance what you do in the course of your day. (Get the kids ready for school, go to work, talk to people, go shopping and cook?) Pay attention not only to your movements but also to your energy as you go through these motions. Do you feel centered or pulled apart? Are you enjoying yourself or not? Are you in giving mode most of the time or do you also receive? Can you find the essence of you at the core of all that activity?

- *Do a dance of compassion for who you are today.* Create a loving dance based on exactly who you are today and where you are in your life. Be careful not to judge what's going on in your life. Just be with what it is and make a point of appreciating all of the factors that created who you are in this moment.

- *Be an animal.* This is an old improvisational standby but still a good one. Become a bird, monkey, cat, wolf, lion and/or snake. Inhabit the spirit of each animal. Which animal best expresses your soul? Becoming an animal helps you transcend some of the trappings of being human.

- *Use masks.* Wear a mask or veil that fully or partially conceals your iden-tity and dance the spirit of that masked persona.

- *Use props.* Use a very simple prop (a pole, a veil, a fan, a basket or a ball). In your mind, turn it into a symbol of something else and dance with it. Make your images clear enough so that others could figure out what it is.

- *Do a mirror dance.* Find a partner and mirror each other's moves. Aim to get to a place in which you cannot determine who's leading whom.

- *Carry on a dance conversation.* With one or more partners, begin with a movement phrase. Let your partner or partners respond. Notice when you're in agreement or argument. Notice what you do while the other is talking. Are you both talking at once or are you both listening and adding to the conversation? Sometimes it helps to use music with very obvious breaks and set boundaries for where to begin and end so that one person doesn't take over the conversation. (African and Middle Eastern music commonly use such "call and response" structures.)

You can also create whole dances around simple actions or gestures. Try both the grand gestures that express colossal themes and the everyday gestures that express the fine points of your humanity:

Grand gestures

Praying

Being grateful

Looking within

Searching

Finding

Letting go

Sharing

Opening your heart

Guiding

Being guided

Blessing

Being blessed

Offering

Receiving

Casting out

Forgiving

Being a goddess or god

Everyday gestures

Bathing

Combing your hair, putting on makeup

Singing

Holding a baby

Cooking

Eating, tasting

Sweeping

Sewing

Drawing

Caressing a lover

Daydreaming

Playing an instrument

Saying hello or goodbye

Let Your Habits and Passions Feed Each Other

If you move your body or you diet simply to "lose weight" or "look good," you'll inevitably get bored, rebel and get frustrated that it doesn't work. But if you cultivate your passion to move, you won't have to force yourself to do it and you'll eat healthy foods and do your supplemental workouts with much more enthusiasm—because they support your passion! So you might as well let yourself be at least a little wild and free and use your workout time as an opportunity to surrender to the passion of being alive. The more love you pour into your practice, the more love will in turn start pouring into and out of you.

And so with passion flowing through our veins, let's move on into a very critical territory for women . . . the land of food and hormones.

Creating Internal Balance

8   Eating for Equilibrium

Female bodies seem to thrive on several small meals, spaced evenly throughout the day. We don't function well when we let ourselves get too hungry, then overeat, or eat too much of one sort of food—especially too much or too little fat, carbs or protein. Although this may come as a surprise, one of the biggest mistakes women make is we don't eat *often enough*. As we get older, our metabolism slows down (largely due to lack of exercise) and our waistlines thicken (especially after menopause). Then we tend to eat less because we're not so hungry or don't want to put on more weight. If we eat only one or two meals a day, we slow our metabolism even more, feel sluggish and we don't take in the nutrients our bodies need. The most sensible eating plan for women approaching, in the thick of, or leaving middle age should look something like this:

- *Eat four to five small meals throughout the day*—about 400 to 500 calories every few hours. Anything more than that in one sitting, even in the form of nonfat food, will get stored as fat. (It's important to remember, however, that fat isn't all bad. You need *some* fat to keep nerves and skin healthy. But most of us don't use all that we've got!)

Aim to eat 1,600 to 2,500 calories a day (the more physically active you are, the more you should eat!), consisting of 40 to 50 percent carbohydrates, 25 to 30 percent protein, 25 to 30 percent fat.

Frequent smaller meals will keep your energy level constant, stabilize moods, improve concentration and athletic performance. When you go out to eat, get in the habit of eating half the entrée and taking the other half home. Try to eat most of your food in the daylight hours. Perhaps you've heard that lunch should be your biggest meal of the day. It's true that lunch is important. But it's easy to take this advice the wrong way. A big lunch, especially a carbohydrate-rich meal like a big plate of pasta, can put you right to sleep. If you want to stay mentally alert in the afternoon, eat a *small* plate of pasta and add some slivers of low-fat protein, like chicken or turkey breast. If you can't eat dinner until late in the evening, eat something light (a salad and a baked potato, for example), which is easier to digest overnight than protein. Carbs at night will help you sleep. If you need a snack before bed, try a few graham crackers and warm vanilla soymilk with cinnamon and nutmeg.

- *Choose proteins wisely.* Your body needs protein to repair and rebuild virtually all the tissue in your body. Protein also regulates blood sugar levels and helps you (via a hormone called glucogen) convert stored fats into fuel. Still, you need to choose your protein sources wisely. Animal protein that's high in fat and cholesterol will clog arteries and, over time, increase your risk of heart disease. High-fat meat and dairy products also contain the highest concentrations of xenoestrogens (toxic estrogens found in pesticides, described in the next chapter, which can promote breast and ovarian cancer). If you eat animal protein, eat "organic" poultry, eggs and beef as often as possible and eat fish (especially cold water fish such as salmon). There is some debate about whether or not eating animal protein causes bone loss. To digest animal protein, the stomach secretes a certain acid thought to pull calcium from the bones during the process. Vegetarian sources of protein don't require that same acid in order to be digested, so there's less risk of bone loss.

- *Eat more soy products and vegetable proteins.* Beans and grains complement each other to provide an easily assimilated and digested form of protein. They also contain natural forms of estrogen called phytoestrogens. (*Phyto* means plant. These estrogens are described in detail in the next chapter.) Of all the plant proteins, soybeans contain the most concentrated amount of phytoestrogens. Although the amount is minute (about 1/50,000 the potency of synthetic hormones[1]), it's still capable of binding to our estrogen receptor cells. Like keys opening a lock, these phytoestrogens then balance hormones by raising a low estrogen level or lowering a high one. Perhaps *because* the potency of these phytoestrogens is so mild, our bodies metabolize this form of estrogen much more efficiently than those found in synthetic hormones.

- *Don't overeat carbs.* If you snack on bagels, crackers and nonfat cookies but still feel hungry, sluggish and can't lose fat, eat fewer carbohydrates and more healthy fats and protein. The reason? Even carbs such as white rice and potatoes have a "high glycemic index," which means they're high in sugar. Eating lots of carbohydrates can stimulate the production of insulin (a hormone that promotes fat production), which in turn can cause the carb calories that would normally produce energy to get stored as fat. To balance your system, choose beans or yams, which have a lower glycemic index, or eat a smaller portion of higher glycemic carbs with protein and fat. (Exercise also regulates insulin levels.)

- *Get your essential fatty acids.* The central nervous, immune and cardiovascular systems all need essential fatty acids to function properly. Nutrient-dense fats from the "omega family" can ease PMS and menopausal symptoms, depression, add luster to hair, skin, nails—and help you lose weight! When the body is no longer starved of these nutrients, it more willingly transforms its stored fat into energy. Good sources of omega 3's are cold water fish (salmon, freshwater trout, sardines), flaxseed oil, canola oil, walnuts and pumpkin seeds. Olive oil, sesame oil, avocados and nuts such as almonds and hazelnuts supply omega 9's. You can eat approximately 1000 milligrams per day of omega 3's but just a tablespoon of the tastier omega 9's. When possible eat fresh (not smoked) fish, buy cold-pressed virgin oils and eat only raw, dry-roasted and unsalted nuts. Avoid peanuts.

- *Eliminate margarine and other trans fatty acids.* Highly processed fats like margarine or heated oils (which are often added to muffins and cook-

---

1. Lark, Susan M., *The Women's Health Companion* (Berkeley, CA: Celestial Arts, 1996) http://www.healthy.net/library/books/lark/fdstoeat.htm, 6.

ies) can actually prevent the transformation of the healthy omegas into energy-rich essential fatty acids. The result? More fat on you.

- *Cut back on caffeine.* Drink decaf to minimize PMS and menopausal symptoms. Avoid sodas with caffeine and *all* carbonated beverages because they contain phosphates, which leach calcium from the bones. Beware, too, of sugar substitutes found in soft drinks, since long-term use of these sweeteners is suspected of causing an increase in the growth of cancerous tumors.

- *Eat chocolate wisely.* Chocolate contains caffeine and another caffeine-like substance called theobromine. Both are drugs and should be used wisely. Chocolate is an antidepressant and a little piece of it at the lowest ebb of your menstrual cycle can release endorphins into your system and make you feel better immediately. But chocolate is also high in sugar, fat and calories—and too much can make PMS and mood swings worse! I've found that when I maintain a largely vegetarian, low-fat diet and avoid sweets, alcohol and high-fat foods, I don't crave chocolate as much as I used to. When you must eat chocolate, eat a small piece of the very best you can buy and thoroughly enjoy it!

- *Don't drink alcohol every day.* Even just one beer or glass of wine every night with dinner is *not* good for you, despite what various studies say about the "calming" and "longevity-enhancing" effects of moderate amounts of alcohol. Don't kid yourself. Dr. Andrew Weil points out in *Natural Health, Natural Medicine,* that many such studies are funded by liquor companies. He also tells his patients who like to drink to have two or three alcohol-free days per week.[2] Alcohol, he says, is "poisonous to nerve and liver cells, irritating to the upper digestive tract and urinary system" and in women "may be a significant risk factor for breast cancer."[3] It also "burns up B-vitamins," and, because alcohol contains "empty (carb) calories," when you drink alcohol and eat at the same time, the body uses the alcohol calories immediately and tends to store the food calories as fat.[4] Alcohol also causes sleep disorders, "aggravates biological depression, suppresses ovarian function and diminishes the production of endorphins (the body's natural painkillers)."[5] When you drink, avoid

2. Weil, Andrew, *Natural Health, Natural Medicine* (Boston and New York: Houghton Mifflin, 1995), 136.
3. Ibid., 136.
4. Ibid., 137.
5. Ibid., 137.

hard liquor and choose microbrewed beer or wine with the least amount of added chemicals. Eat protein when you indulge and cut back on carbs.

A Closer Look at Soy

Soy is finally starting to get the attention it deserves. Soy is a wonder-food—especially for women. Here's what it can do.

Eating soy can regulate hormone balance. Only 10 to 15 percent of all Japanese women suffer from menopausal hot flashes (they don't even have a word for this condition in Japan), but 80 to 85 percent of American women get them.[6] Why the difference? Japanese women eat much less meat and dairy and much more *soy*, grains, beans and vegetables. Western women who maintain a vegetarian diet closer to the Japanese diet eliminate two to three times more "spent" estrogen through their bowels than meat eaters do.[7] In other words, a vegetarian diet seems to inspire already used estrogens to pass through the system more efficiently, preventing problems caused by too much estrogen (a situation some doctors call "estrogen dominance"—explained in the next chapter). Dr. Susan Love, the author of *Dr. Susan Love's Hormone Book*, says that the phytoestrogens in soy and other plant foods may even help lengthen the first ("feel good") part of the menstrual cycle by three to four days—and minimize some PMS symptoms by decreasing the amount of ("don't feel so good") hormones that get secreted at ovulation, which later cause a drop in energy and shift in mood.[8]

Eating soy might prevent cancer. The U.S. Soyfoods Directory says that one serving a day of soy may also be enough to protect against cancer,[9] since soy contains antioxidants, those "fighting" cells that defend against the proliferation of free radicals (dangerous chemicals, often caused by oxidized polyunsaturated fats that can damage DNA, cause the formation of malignant cells and weaken the immune system). People who eat soy on a regular basis have lower incidences of endometrial, ovarian, colon and prostate cancers. Because soy regulates hormone levels, it also decreases the cancer risks associated with high levels of estrogen, namely breast and uterine cancers.

6. Vliet, Elizabeth Lee, *Screaming to Be Heard: Hormonal Connections Women Suspect and Doctors Ignore* (New York: M. Evans and Co.), 246.
7. Lark, Susan M., *The Women's Health Companion*, http://www.healthy.net/library/books/lark/fdstoeat.htm, 2.
8. Love, Susan M., and Lindsey, Karen, *Dr. Susan Love's Hormone Book* (New York: Random House, 1997), 197.
9. U.S. Soyfoods Directory, www.soyfoods.com/nutrition/nutrition.html

Dr. Love cites some other ways soy appears to fight cancer:

- it appears to prevent tumors in rats who've had their ovaries removed,

- it blocks an enzyme (called tyrosine kinase) that is otherwise friendly to cancer cells,

- it prevents new blood vessel growth inside breast cancer tumors and

- it may be especially good for girls and young women since it helps maturing breast cells become more resistant to cancer.[10]

Eating soy may prevent heart disease. A study out of the University of Kentucky and the VA Medical Center (which examined the findings from thirty-eight studies on soy) suggests that two servings of soy a day might lower cholesterol by 7 to 10 percent—and reduce the risk of heart disease by 15 to 25 percent![11] Soy not only *lowers* bad cholesterol (the LDLs, or low-density lipoproteins) but also *raises* good cholesterol (the HDLs, or high-density lipoproteins)—not significantly, but a little (the average was 2.4 percent). Since every single percentage point drop in total cholesterol decreases the risk of heart attack by 2 to 3 percent, two doses of soy per day could reduce the risk of heart attack by 18 to 28 percent![12]

Soy may also inhibit blood clots (which can lead to stroke) and reduce the growth of plaque cells that line and clog arteries (which increase the risk of heart disease and heart attack). This is especially important for women who go through menopause, since the drop in artery- and heart-protecting estrogen typically and suddenly predisposes women to both heart attacks and stroke.

Eating soy may prevent osteoporosis. Soy protects bones in a number of ways:

1. It's high in calcium.

2. Unlike animal protein, which may leach calcium from bones during digestion, soy does not.

3. It may actually stop bone deterioration.

4. It may increase bone mineral density.

10. Love, Susan M., and Lindsay, Karen, *Dr. Susan Love's Hormone Book*, 197.
11. Anderson, James W., M.D., Metabolic Research Group, VA Medical Center and U. of Kentucky, www.ag.uiuc.edu/~stratsoy/soyhealth.html.
12. Ibid.

Soy is about 40 percent high-quality protein, with eight of the essential amino acids, mandatory for building and repairing tissue. Most importantly, it provides protein without the threat of bone loss. (The stomach doesn't secrete the same acid to digest soy as it does to digest animal protein.) In fact, soy may even help the bones *retain* calcium. A standard serving of soy also contains about one-third the calcium of a comparable serving of milk, so it's a relatively high-calcium food.

The long-standing debate about how much protein our bodies really need rages on. Although the RDA for protein is only 15 percent of total calories, advocates of higher protein diets have made convincing arguments in favor of more protein and fewer carbs. Meanwhile many other nutritionists still point out that too much protein can cause bone loss.

No one knows yet for sure, but the real culprit causing bone loss may not be too *much* protein but the type of protein. In *Dr. Susan Love's Hormone Book*, Dr. Love cites a study of meat-eating versus vegetarian women. Those who "ate meat regularly lost 35 percent of their bone mass between ages 50 and 89, while vegetarians who ate eggs and dairy products lost only 18 percent, even though both groups had the same amount of calcium in their diets. Another study found that vegetarians had higher bone density at age 70 than meat eaters at age 50."[13] Neither of these studies took a close look at the value of soy. But they did make a strong case for vegetarianism (and soy is a typical staple in a vegetarian diet).

We still don't know all there is to know about preventing osteoporosis. Paradoxically, Asian women (with their vegetarian diets that supposedly prevent bone loss) and Caucasian women (who tend to favor meat and dairy) are both at higher risk for the disease than women of other cultural backgrounds are. At this point, researchers haven't determined if Asian women are at higher risk for osteoporosis because they have "small bones" or because western influence has started to alter their diets to include more meat and dairy and fewer plant products. But Asian women have far fewer *fractures* than Caucasians. If it turns out that a vegetarian diet high in soy doesn't ultimately protect against osteoporosis but does prevent fractures, then it's doing an important job. Many women with osteoporosis live active lives—*until* they break a bone. Every year, 20 percent of all women who break a hip die of complications within three months and 50 percent never walk again.[14]

---

13. Love, Susan M., and Lindsey, Karen, *Dr. Susan Love's Hormone Book*, 195.
14. Vliet, Elizabeth Lee, *Screaming to Be Heard*, 17.

Incidentally, aside from being Caucasian or Asian, the risk factors for osteoporosis include:

- A family history of the disease

- Being prematurely gray

- Being small-boned

- Being inactive (taking no weight-bearing exercise, such as weight lifting; dancing; walking or yoga)

- Chronic dieting

- Smoking cigarettes

- Drinking caffeinated drinks and carbonated sodas

- Taking birth control pills

- Being excessively, obsessively physically active. Some ballet dancers and gymnasts, who may look like the picture of physical fitness, actually experience bone loss in their youth (or set themselves up for it later). A combination of heavy training and dieting (especially when they have such low body fat they miss their periods), smoking, drinking coffee and, God forbid, getting addicted to drugs like cocaine or heroin all damage bones at an early age.

Eating soy may promote weight loss. Is soy a good food for weight loss? That depends. Soy is by nature a low-fat food. Three ounces of "average" tofu contains about 50 calories—20 of which come from fat (10 percent of which is saturated). The same amount of tempeh (cultured soy food) has about 150 calories, 40 from fat. You can buy low-fat versions of both tofu and tempeh with half the amount of fat. Be vigilant about reading the label on soy *burgers.* Some carry a walloping nine to fifteen grams of fat per serving! Many others are very low in fat—and are still tasty.

Overall, soy *is* a good food for weight loss since it's low in saturated fat, high in fiber and bulky, so it fills you up. Also, if you're health-conscious enough to eat soy, you're probably also conscious enough to exercise, eat your vegetables and avoid too many sweets and high-fat foods.

A global benefit of eating soy and other legumes and grains is that it helps save the planet. Overgrazing by cattle has contributed to a significant loss of grasses and other green plants that supply oxygen and keep our planet livable. If we all ate less meat and more legumes and grains, we wouldn't need to breed so much livestock and therefore wouldn't create so much ecological damage caused by overgrazing. Feeding the ever-growing world population would also be a far less daunting task since more healthy plant-foods would feed *people* instead of livestock.

So How Do You Like Your Soy?

Tofu, that poor maligned little bean curd and the butt of so many anti-New Age jokes, is just one of many tasty "meat replacement" products made of soy. These days you can slip soy into just about any recipe and not only fool but satisfy even the most rugged carnivores.

You should be aware that foods like tofu, tempeh, soymilk, miso and soy flour, which go through the *least* amount of processing, contain the *most* phytoestrogens and antioxidants—in other words, they're the best ones for you. More highly processed foods, like soy ice cream or soy sausages, are less potent because they have less soy and a greater percentage of other ingredients. Soy sauce and soy oil, incidentally, contain *no* phytoestrogens—and neither does margarine made from soy oil.

To get the most mileage from soy, plan to eat—or *drink*—your soy in the morning *and* at night, since phytoestrogens pass out of the system after about eight hours. Don't worry about eating "too much" soy. It can't hurt. It's high in fiber, low in saturated fat and contains omega-3 fatty acids, which help lower cholesterol. The worst thing that can happen if you eat too much soy is gas (and a little Beano before you eat can fix that).

In case you've never been a vegetarian or haven't shopped in the health food store or section of your supermarket lately, here's a quick review of your soy choices:

Tofu. This soybean cake, although bland by itself, is actually a very accommodating food, absorbing any flavor you put with it. Slice it, cube it, mash it with herbs and garlic to make a dip, liquify it and turn it into a salad dressing.

Tempeh. Much tastier than tofu, this cultured soy product is nutty and chewy. Delicious sautéed with vegetables and served over rice with a tasty sauce. Also good garnished with lettuce, tomato and fancy mustard and cradled in a bun.

Soy burgers. A mix of tempeh, tofu and mashed-up grains. Be sure to read the fat grams! But even the low-fat ones can be very satisfying. You can also find soy hot dogs, sausage and bacon. Just remember, the greater the amount of processing, the weaker the phytoestrogens.

Miso. This soybean paste comes in many colors—white, yellow, red and brown. Delicious smeared on a sandwich, watered down with scallions and tofu and simmered in soup, also perfect with vegetable broth as a base for a sauté sauce.

Soy flour. Use it in place of some of the regular flour in breads, muffins, pancakes and so on.

Soy protein powder. Many health food stores sell this cheaply in bulk. You don't *have* to buy the expensive versions with extra-added vitamins and minerals.

Soymilk. Ah, my lifeblood! Eight ounces of "regular" whole soymilk has about 140 calories and four grams of fat per serving (it can also be very thick). "Lite," or low-fat, soymilk has about 120 calories and two grams of fat—and it's creamy and satisfying. Nonfat soymilk has 90 calories and zero fat but is as tasty as yellow dishwater. I recommend the low-fat vanilla. Many companies make it. Mix with Chai (spicy Indian tea) for a tasty coffee substitute.

Eat More Grains and Beans

Whole grains (as opposed to processed white flour products—i.e., pasta and bread) served together with beans (black, soy, etc.) and/or nuts form complete proteins—or all essential amino acids. (By themselves, they're missing a few essential amino acids.) They're also high in nutrients, fiber, vitamins, minerals and phytoestrogens. Eating more whole grains and beans doesn't mean you have to spend more time cooking. You can cook grains (such as millet, amaranth and Arborio rice) easily in a rice cooker and store in the fridge to use later. You can buy canned beans (look for ones that claim to use no pesticides) or, if you cook your own, soak them overnight in plenty of water (and remove any pebbles that have sneaked in). Rinse. Cover with fresh water (add spices, onions, garlic and other flavorings). Bring to a boil and cook until tender, an hour or so. To store them for a long time, put them in freezer bags and freeze. When you're ready to use them, thaw the bag in the microwave or put bag into warm water before you cook.

To form complete proteins, mix your grains, beans and nuts. There's no end to the combinations. Try:

Arborio rice (a plump, sweet rice) and black beans

Millet and almonds (with soymilk!)

Barley and kidney bean soup

Whole wheat bread, almonds, a banana and raisins

So What's on the Menu?

The following menu suggestions are so easy, you don't need recipes. To eat for equilibrium, remember to eat a variety of foods, eat breakfast, eat your veggies, eat every four hours, don't overindulge in carbohydrates (simple or complex), drink lots of water and balance your nutrients between carbs, protein and essential fats. The following simple meal ideas can help balance your energy and hormones.

Breakfast choices

Chai and low-fat vanilla soymilk

1 cup reheated grains, with soymilk, cinnamon, maple syrup and gomasio (sesame seasoning)

Scrambled eggs or tofu in olive oil with tomatoes, avocado and toast

Low-fat cottage cheese with fruit on 1 waffle or pancake

1 cup of cereal and soymilk

Midmorning snack

Fruit smoothie with soy protein powder

Lunch choices

Soy or turkey burger

Tofu, chicken or fish taco with beans

Salad with tempeh or tofu and crackers

Tofu chili and corn tortillas

Vegetable miso soup and half a turkey sandwich

Midafternoon snack

Almond butter or avocado on 1 piece of toast

The other half of your turkey sandwich and an apple

Dinner choices

Stir-fried vegetables with tofu or chicken and sesame seeds over $1/2$ cup of rice

Tofu or turkey lasagne

Grilled salmon, green veggies and 2 new potatoes

Shepherd's pie with garbanzos, grains and/or tofu. Top with a "crust" of mashed potatoes and yams (mash with soymilk, add herbs for flavor)

Maintaining Nutritional Balance

Maintaining balance with food is about as challenging as it is with exercise. No one can keep up the same regimen all the time. Holidays, vacations, illness, work, family obligations or just boredom all have a way of wreaking havoc with your best intentions. Besides, we all need to enjoy our food more. Eat big meals when you need them and really savor them without guilt. As you commit to living in balance, you'll get better at reading your body's signals and knowing what types and amounts of foods make you feel your best.

But even your best intentions won't prevent the wild dragon inside you from occasionally running out of its cave and blowing fire on everyone in its path. Hormones taking you on a wild ride? Read on. . . .

9   Taming the Dragon

Our brain and hormones conspire to create a certain interval during each month when we are neurophysically less available for joy and more tuned in to the release of difficult emotions that may have been building up all month. This emotional housecleaning is wrongly viewed as bitchiness or complaining, but when seen rightly and heeded, it may be a valuable stress reducer and guide to what we need to change or pay attention to so our lives will run more smoothly. This is the benefit of feeling down. —JOAN BORYSENKO, *A WOMAN'S BOOK OF LIFE*

Premenstrually, we are quite naturally more "in tune" with what is most meaningful in our lives. We're more apt to cry but our tears are always related to something that holds meaning for us. . . . To the extent that we are out of touch with hidden parts of ourselves, we will suffer premenstrually. Years of personal and clinical experience have taught me that the painful or uncomfortable issues that arise premenstrually are always real and must be addressed. —CHRISTIANE NORTHRUP, *WOMEN'S BODIES, WOMEN'S WISDOM*

It's relatively easy to balance ourselves with exercise and eating well but finding hormonal balance is another matter. When it comes to hormones, it often feels like Nature has played a practical joke on women. Is this the way it's supposed to be?

Have we been "genetically programmed" to get worse PMS as we get older—especially if we don't have children or have them late in life? Is this some form of punishment for not breeding soon enough or at all? What's the purpose of that sometimes ten-year-long, nebulous hormonal roller coaster ride called perimenopause? Must we go through such a long process to "get in touch with" our vulnerability? Is this nature's way of forcing us onto a more spiritual path? And why, after menopause, do we lose the protective shield of estrogen—so we can die off sooner of heart disease, cancer and osteoporosis—just when we're starting to get wise? Did Nature really intend us to solve these problems by using our *intelligence* to manufacture pharmaceuticals? Or have we landed in this mess because of processed foods; high-fat, high-protein diets; inactive lifestyles and our own negative beliefs about our menstrual experiences?

Whatever the cause, reassuring information has begun to surface that indicates that we *may* be able to solve some of our hormonal imbalances simply by adjusting what we eat, what activities we do, what type of hormones we take, if any, and also, perhaps, what we *believe.*

I got interested in hormonal problems because, like many women in their late thirties and early forties, my body at this age started to go haywire. I had never before had bad PMS or difficult menstrual periods. Now suddenly PMS lasted two weeks and I often had to spend the first day of my period in bed. But then there were easy months with no symptoms at all, which made my body seem even more unpredictable and out of control.

I'm ambitious, have a lot of responsibilities and tend to drive myself pretty hard. At first, I resented the way my period took me "out of the race." Later, I began to realize that my body, in its compassionate wisdom, gave me PMS and immobilizing cramps *because* I drove myself so hard. There was no other way I'd let myself lie in a fetal position for that long. Now that I let myself rest, eat more soy and do more yoga, I actually *look forward* to the insights my period affords me—and my PMS symptoms and menstrual cramps have gotten much easier.

Like millions of women in my generation, I was never taught to associate menstruation with anything positive—except that it meant my body was functioning normally and I wasn't pregnant. It was still called "the curse" when I was growing up. I remember being herded into the cafeteria with all the other little girls in the fifth grade, where the school nurse showed us a slide show about ovaries and so on and passed around a Kotex napkin as big as a shoe. The whole thing seemed foul and humiliating. We learned that when we got our periods we could skip recess if we wanted to and should probably stay out of the pool. We didn't hear anything about birth control or how this initiation into womanhood also ushered in a "magic time."

Christiane Northrup writes in her excellent book, *Women's Bodies, Women's Wisdom*, that premenstrually and during menstruation, "women are most in tune with their inner knowing and with what isn't working in their lives." It's the time when the "veil between the worlds of the seen and unseen, the conscious and unconscious, is much thinner . . . when we have greater access to our magic—our ability to change things for the better."[1] Native American women, she writes, used to go into a "moon lodge" with other menstruating women to

---

1. Northrup, Christiane, *Women's Bodies, Women's Wisdom: Creating Physical and Emotional Health and Healing* (New York: Bantam Books, 1994), 101.

have "visioning" experiences and would emerge afterward, "inspired and also inspiring to others."[2] She believes that if we could just take three or four days a month to go within and have our meals brought to us by someone else(!), "the majority of PMS cases would disappear.[3] We'd look forward to this time, instead of dreading it (I know I would!). Perhaps it'll take a few generations before women restructure the world so it honors our cycles this way.

But before we can fully change the world, we have to examine our *perceptions* about our entire menstrual experience—from our first period to our last. Although there are huge numbers of women now actively engaged in managing their menopausal symptoms with exercise, eating right and educating themselves about hormones, there's still a lot of negative talk about PMS and menstruation among those of us who still bleed. I'm guilty of it. I used to say, "Watch out, I'm very PMS today" or "I hate my period," and I've often heard other women say similar things. I'm earnestly trying to weed out these negative words and instead say something like "it's the inward time of the month for me" or "my body needs to rest today." By changing my words, I've changed how I think about my entire menstrual experience. Perhaps if *more* of us change our perceptions and maintain habits that support our internal balance, we can begin to put an end to our widespread hormonal struggles and instead celebrate the entire reproductive cycle and truly absorb the wisdom it affords us.

Hormones 101

To learn full compassion for our cycles and appreciate this great miracle that goes on in our bodies throughout much of our lives, it helps to understand what our sex hormones do and how they affect us.

Hormones move through the bloodstream like keys ready to open specific locks (i.e., specific organs, "receptor" cells or "host sites"). Once the hormones open the right door, a floodgate of chemical information, which has been wired into that site, pours out. We then respond to this chemical reaction in a number of ways: we run away, sleep, digest different nutrients, become aroused, get pregnant, become euphoric, cranky, violent and so forth.

Once the "messenger hormone" does its job, it either gets eliminated through the blood, urine or feces or it moves along to a "recycling center" in the body, where it's used like a "starter" for a new batch of hormones (the body is so elegantly efficient!). When everything goes smoothly, this hormone–receptor cell

2. Ibid., 103.
3. Ibid., 103.

tango puts us in homeostasis or "internal balance." But without the right hormones, the right *mix* of hormones, the proper flushing of spent hormones, or due to some malfunction of the messenger or host cells, the body goes out of balance.

We have *some* control over our hormonal secretions. When we relax, exercise, meditate, eat certain foods, laugh, flirt or make love, we release a tide of "happy hormones." When we're frightened, overwhelmed, overworked and the like, we release stress hormones. When we "stuff" our emotions and even mask them behind various addictions, we secrete yet other types of hormones (called enkephalins) that actually suppress our desire to shed tears.[4] (As Christiane Northrup says, "tears contain toxins that the body needs to get rid of. Tears of joy and tears of sorrow have different chemical compositions and are influenced by hormones. They also serve different purposes."[5] Both allow us to feel and release emotions. Insights usually come *after* we shed our tears.)

What we think, eat and do affects which hormones we secrete just as much as hormone secretion affects our thoughts, desires and actions. It's a two-way street. But when it comes to sex hormones, we don't have as much direct control. Our female hormones in particular are very busy every month overseeing the process of "egg production," fertilization or menstruation. From the first day of our periods up until ovulation (about fourteen days later) our follicles (little sacs that prepare and hold our eggs) produce estrogen (in what's called the "follicular phase"). Once the follicles are stimulated, one "lucky" follicle is chosen to prepare and deliver an egg—and estrogen levels peak at this time. When estrogen levels are high, we feel good and full of energy.

After ovulation, estrogen levels start to drop because it's no longer being produced in the follicles. The follicle that produced the egg then transforms itself into another little sac, the corpus luteum (or "little yellow body"), which then produces progesterone, the other "female" hormone. Progesterone prepares the body for pregnancy and has a sedative effect. Immediately after ovulation, estrogen levels start to plummet and progesterone rises, peaking in the middle of the second half of our cycle (around day 21 or 22 of a twenty-eight-day cycle—PMS time). We have higher levels of progesterone than estrogen at this time. After day 22, progesterone starts to drop and stays low (unless we're pregnant) until the first day of the period, when *both* progesterone and estrogen are low—although estrogen at this point is somewhat higher than progesterone.

And so it goes, from our first period to our last. During our menstrual years,

4. Ibid., 55.
5. Ibid., 55.

we're always on some part of the menstrual wheel. We've been hormonally pro-gramed to move forward, build, create and conquer the world in the two weeks prior to ovulation and then step back in the two weeks before menstruation to process what we've gained and prepare to flush out what we no longer need.

Estrogens Are Not All Alike

I'm ashamed to admit that until recently, I thought there was just one type of estrogen. But, in fact, there are three kinds that we make in our bodies, two types we ingest in our foods and several types that we can get by prescription. Each of us has different amounts of these various estrogens, depending on our genes, our age, how many pregnancies we've had (or if we've not had any), how much fat we carry and what we eat. Before menopause, we mostly manufacture estrogen in our ovaries. After menopause, we produce it in our body fat and other organs—but at only 40 to 60 percent of the amount we had in our twenties.[6]

17-beta estradiol is the dominant estrogen—the one that gives us breasts, soft faces and menstrual cycles. Its over four hundred functions include pro-tecting bones, heart, nerves, enhancing memory, regulating moods and sleep. After menopause, this is the type of estrogen that plummets. With a drop in 17-beta estradiol, after menopause, women's risk for heart disease and osteoporo-sis rises considerably. Low levels of 17-beta estradiol also create memory loss, vaginal dryness, drier skin, thinner hair, and disrupted sleep—not as serious perhaps but these things definitely affect our sense of self and quality of life.

Some "natural," or plant-based, estrogen replacement medications (as opposed to pharmaceutically created estrogens) mimic human estradiol and offer some of its heart and bone protection. These include Estrace (tablets and cream), Climara (a skin patch) and Estraderm (another patch)—and are avail-able by prescription.[7]

Estrone is the second most dominant estrogen. It actually helps the body pro-duce 17-beta estradiol. After menopause, estrone becomes the *dominant* estrogen and is primarily manufactured in body fat. Women with high levels of body fat, therefore, tend to have higher levels of estrone. Many medical specialists suspect that high levels of estrone may be responsible for the increased risk of cancers after menopause. Thus, maintaining a moderate level of body fat may prevent cancers

6. Borysenko, Joan, *A Woman's Book of Life: The Biology, Psychology, and Spirituality of the Feminine Life Cycle* (New York: Riverhead Books, 1997), 176.
7. Vliet, Elizabeth Lee, *Screaming to Be Heard: Hormonal Connections Women Suspect and Doctors Ignore* (New York: M. Evans and Co.), 98.

caused by estrone. Premarin, the popular estrogen replacement drug, is estrone.

Estriol is an estrogen produced in highest amounts during pregnancy. It's thought to be the weakest of the estrogens and doesn't protect bones and the heart the way estradiol does. However, estriol is believed to help the body synthesize, use and break down the other two types of estrogen. When the two stronger estrogens don't get naturally flushed through the system, they build up and create an imbalance, or "estrogen dominance." Health problems arise from having too *much* estrogen as well as from too little. Some of the problems associated with too much estrogen include:

- Increased risk of breast cancer
- Bone loss
- Loss of vascular tone (the vessels going to and from the heart)
- Greater tendency for blood clots (which increase the risk of stroke)
- Thyroid problems
- Loss of interest in sex
- Depression
- Heavy menstrual flow
- Headaches

Estriol isn't available in prescription or nonprescription form in the United States but is used in some postmenopausal medications in Europe.

ESTROGENS WE EAT

Phytoestrogens are organic, plant-based, estrogen-like compounds found in soy and other beans, whole grains, nuts, yams, also the herbs ginseng, black cohosh and dong quai. The estrogen in these foods is estriol—in very minute doses—which binds to the same estrogen receptor cells as the estrogens in our bodies do. In *Dr. Susan Love's Hormone Book*, Dr. Love writes, "[Phytoestrogens] have the interesting ability to raise a low level of estrogen but lower a high level [by replacing a strong estrogen with a weaker one]. Because of this [phytoestrogens] are often known as 'balancers.' In a pre-menopausal woman, they decrease estrogen; in a post menopausal woman, they increase it."[8]

8. Love, Susan M., and Lindsey, Karen, *Dr. Susan Love's Hormone Book* (New York: Random House, 1997), 153.

Should women with breast cancer, or at high risk for any cancer, avoid phytoestrogens in case they cause a recurrence or new cancer? Because plant estrogens are so much less potent than synthetic estrogens, there seems to be much less cause for alarm. But, as Dr. Love says, "the answers really are not in yet."[9]

Xenoestrogens are toxic, "foreign" estrogens found in pesticides (such as DDT and PCB's) derived from chlorine and petrochemical derivatives sprayed on animal feed. Animals store these chemicals in their body fat where it seems to gather force and become much more highly concentrated. (Joan Borysenko writes, "Butter has a 2000 percent greater concentration of these pollutants than the grain fed to cows.")[10] Consequently, when we eat the flesh or milk of animals fed xenoestrogens, we then store their xenoestrogens in our body fat! The more fatty the beef or dairy, the greater the amount. High-fat meat and dairy products already cause problems for hearts and bones but the xenoestrogens may also increase the risk for breast and ovarian cancers in women—and promote infertility and low sperm count in men.

SYNTHETIC ESTROGENS

Birth control pills contain some of the most powerful doses of estrogen (in a form similar to 17-beta estradiol). Although doses are lower now than in the past, birth control pills can still upset a woman's hormonal balance and increase the risk of cancer. Dr. Andrew Weil, author and noted advocate of complementary medicine, says he "never prescribes them" and has his female patients stop taking them because of their toxic effects. Dr. Weil also suggests that any woman should stop taking birth control pills who:

- Has a family history of breast cancer

- Has a family history of fibrocystic (benign) breast disease

- Hasn't had a first child before age thirty-five

- Is over forty-five and still menstruating

- Has had multiple sexual partners (and therefore is at increased risk of contracting cervical cancer)[11]

9. Ibid., 153.
10. Borysenko, Joan, *A Woman's Book of Life*, 168.
11. Weil, Andrew, *Natural Health, Natural Medicine* (Boston and New York: Houghton Mifflin, 1995), 172.

Dr. Weil also recommends that women on birth control pills shouldn't smoke, since smoking and the pill together increase the body's tendency to form blood clots, which doubles the risk for having a stroke.

Premarin is by far the drug most prescribed for estrogen replacement therapy. (The name Premarin is derived from the phrase *pregnant mare's urine.*) In *A Woman's Book of Life,* Joan Borysenko writes, "Premarin is produced under intensely inhumane conditions. Pregnant mares are permanently catheterized and confined to a tiny space. After they give birth, they are allowed to nurse their foals for only one week so they can be impregnated again as soon as possible. These living Premarin factories often die during their second or third pregnancy from the stress of confinement."[12] These cruel conditions not only torture the animal, but also no doubt cause the horses to produce high levels of stress hormones, which then end up in our bodies.)

Premarin actually consists of several different (horse) estrogens. Because they're all foreign to the human body, they take longer than "natural" hormones to attach to the receptor sites and can't be metabolized as quickly. According to Dr. Elizabeth Lee Vliet, author of *Screaming to Be Heard,* this might be one reason why women who take Premarin "still have the symptoms of estrogen loss."[13] Dr. Vliet writes, "To date there have not been *any* significant prospective, double-blind controlled studies in the country *comparing* the equine estrogens with the native human estrogen 17-beta estradiol to see whether there are *differences* in side effects, blood pressure changes, breast cancer incidence, uterine cancer rates, brain effects, and/or joint-muscle pain syndromes."[14]

Drug companies can't patent "natural" hormones like the ones in our bodies and in plant foods, so they put their money into researching and manufacturing synthetics—which *can* be patented. As Dr. Susan Love points out, between *one-sixth and one-quarter* of all postmenopausal women in the United States take Premarin! That amounts to 44.3 million prescriptions, which racks up $850 million in sales per year.[15] Obviously, hormone replacement is big business and getting bigger all the time.

12. Borysenko, Joan, *A Woman's Book of Life,* 170.
13. Vliet, Elizabeth Lee, *Screaming to Be Heard,* 35.
14. Ibid., 97.
15. Love, Susan M., and Lindsey, Karen, *Dr. Susan Love's Hormone Book,* 36.

The Other Sex Hormones

Progesterone's whole purpose in life is to prepare a friendly atmosphere for a fertilized egg. Perhaps to make an egg feel "at home," it virtually mimics the first stages of pregnancy, with weight gain, increased appetite, swollen breasts, water retention. It speeds our metabolism but also slows down the passage of food through the intestines, so we want to eat more but we eliminate less and thus feel bloated (all to insure that we'll have enough nutrients to nourish a fetus). Progesterone also affects our insulin levels, so we crave sweets.

If the egg is fertilized, progesterone levels stay high for about two weeks. After that, the placenta starts to manufacture its own progesterone. But when no pregnancy occurs, progesterone levels drop sharply, and it's this drop that causes the thick lining of the uterus to break up and start bleeding.

During the week before and up to the first day of the period, this unique hormone situation puts the immune system at its most vulnerable. In *Ageless Body, Timeless Mind,* Deepak Chopra cites a very interesting study on women who underwent breast cancer surgery. Women who had the surgery at this phase of their cycle were "four times more likely to suffer a recurrence of their disease and to die within ten years than those women who had surgery between day 7 and 20 of their monthly cycle."[16] Chopra says that at midmonth (during ovulation) the "scavenging immune cells" that destroy foreign and malignant cells may be present in full force. This is the best time to schedule surgery.

Progesterone is a natural *tranquilizer.* Although tranquil is not the word that springs to mind for women with PMS, many of us learn to appreciate the sedative effects of progesterone. Progesterone attaches to the same receptor sites in the brain where the antianxiety drugs Valium and Xanax do! In fact, one of the chemical "ingredients" in progesterone is eight times stronger than the most potent of these barbiturates.[17]

As we get older, we ovulate less, even if we still menstruate. When this happens, the corpus luteum doesn't create *any* progesterone. In my research I've found two contradictory descriptions of this. Dr. Elizabeth Lee Vliet says, "In cycles when you do ovulate you will have higher levels of progesterone, and those cycles are usually ones when you have more PMS. . . . In cycles when you don't ovulate, there isn't much progesterone, so you sail through and don't

---

16. Chopra, Deepak, *Ageless Body, Timeless Mind* (New York: Harmony Books, 1993), 144.
17. Vliet, Elizabeth Lee, *Screaming to Be Heard*; 87.

notice any PMS-type changes."[18] On the other hand, Joan Borysenko says, "anovulatory cycles [when you don't ovulate] result in low progesterone relative to estrogen. These are the cycles accompanied by breast tenderness, decreased sex drive, depression, bloating, weight gain, headaches and foggy thinking."[19]

Clearly, it's going to take more time and research to fully understand the balance of hormones and the power of progesterone.

Provera is a synthetic form of progesterone that started to appear on the medical horizon in the early 1980s. After medical professionals discovered that the horse estrogen–based Premarin could increase a woman's risk of cancer, sales dropped. Provera was also developed to counter some of Premarin's negative physical side effects (i.e., uterine cancer and bone loss) and perhaps pump up lagging pharmaceutical company revenues. Provera didn't prove to be a great antidote for Premarin after all—it raises cholesterol.[20] Still, these two drugs were and still are frequently prescribed together, although many women who have taken the "Premarin-Provera recipe" have found that it makes them depressed and crazed. As Gail Sheehy writes in *The Silent Passage:*

"On day fifteen, when I had to add the Provera pills to my regimen, I felt by afternoon as if I had a terrible hangover. This chemically induced state was not to be subdued by aspirin or a walk in the park. It only worsened as the day went on, bringing with it a racing heart, irritability, waves of sadness and difficulty concentrating. And to top it off, the hot flashes came back! Cramps introduced pain for a week at a time. By night I couldn't go to sleep without a glass of wine and even then was awakened by a racing heart and sweating. *Won't I ever be me anymore?* "[21]

Gail Sheehy opted to go cold turkey off both hormones, which put her through a few up-and-down cycles, then she decided to take half her estrogen dose, minus the Provera, which seemed to work. It also gave her the impetus to write her book. Women who go the Premarin-Provera route, as Gail Sheehy did, typically have to fine-tune the amounts of hormones they take to find a balance they can live with.

"Natural" progesterone creams offer a simple, over-the-counter option for women who want to attempt to battle PMS and menopausal symptoms on their

18. Ibid., 52.
19. Borysenko, Joan, *A Woman's Book of Life,* 176.
20. Love, Susan M., and Lindsey, Karen, *Dr. Susan Love's Hormone Book,* 110.
21. Sheehy, Gail, *The Silent Passage* (New York: Random House, 1991), 18–19.

own. "Natural" means that the hormonal makeup of the creams mimics the body's own progesterone, even though it's made from wild yam and/or soybeans. Since this "natural" hormone can't be patented and therefore doesn't generate huge amounts of money for pharmaceutical companies, very little pharmaceutical company research money has been spent testing the value or risks of these creams. Drug companies instead put their money into researching and developing *synthetic* forms of progesterone, like Provera, which *can* be patented.

These "natural" creams *may* also help shrink fibroid tumors and possibly prevent and treat osteoporosis—but these effects aren't definite. They may also counter the effects of "estrogen dominance" and prevent cancers. But, Dr. Susan Love points out, "natural" progesterone may offer some protection against uterine cancer, but may not do the same for breast cancer.[22] There's still much that isn't known.

Of course, if you experiment with these "natural" hormones, it's best to do so under the guidance of your doctor; but that's not always realistic. Since these creams *are* readily available without a prescription, you *can* use them at your own discretion. Progesterone creams are available in health food stores and some drugstores. Doses range from almost no progesterone to about twenty to thirty milligrams per application.[23] With hormones, as with all drugs, vitamins and herbs, you should try to use the *lowest* effective dose. If PMS or menopausal symptoms get worse as you use the cream or increase your dosage, gradually lower your dosage before you stop using the cream.

Dr. Christiane Northrup usually recommends "natural" progesterone for women with "moderate to severe PMS that doesn't respond to simple lifestyle changes" and for women who experience "Jekyll-and-Hyde premenstrual personality changes."[24]

Typically, women should begin using these creams a few days before symptoms would normally occur (usually just before ovulation). Application is easy. Rub the cream where the skin is thinnest (under the arms, on the neck, behind the knees, etc.). The progesterone is then absorbed into the body fat and from there it travels into the blood, without being processed by the liver. This is a safer way for the body to absorb it.

Testosterone—as surprising as it may be—it is yet another sex hormone women produce in the ovaries. (Men, of course, produce this in their testi-

---

22. Love, Susan M., and Lindsey, Karen, *Dr. Susan Love's Hormone Book,* 116.
23. Ibid., 177.
24. Northrup, Christiane, *Women's Bodies, Women's Wisdom,* 124.

cles.) Before menopause, women have about one-fifteenth the amount of testosterone that men do. After menopause, our testosterone levels increase *twentyfold*,[25] thus heralding in a time when we may become what Joan Borysenko calls "the Guardian," when we are most assertive and feel drawn to work for humanity at large. Testosterone increases our sex drive and energy and also makes muscles and bones stronger. But in order for testosterone to work its positive medicine, there has to be enough 17-beta estradiol in the system. (Estrogen, like a good hostess, helps the testosterone bind to its receptor sites.)

Women with high levels of testosterone, however, share many male health problems. They grow more facial hair, have deeper voices and typically notice that their figures switch from pear to apple-shaped. Blood pressure and cholesterol levels typically rise and so does the risk of heart disease. Women often compound these risks by exercising less and eating more.

But postmenopausal women can also have *low* testosterone, especially after a hysterectomy—which can decrease sex drive, cause fatigue, shrink muscles and weaken bones. Taking doctor-prescribed testosterone can solve these problems without producing masculine features because the doses are very low. (Dr. Elizabeth Lee Vliet prescribes testosterone for women, in one-fifth to one-eighth the amount prescribed for men. Testosterone comes in several forms: "micronized" particles, which can pass through the digestive process, also creams, gels, sublinguals [under the tongue] and suppositories.) However, Dr. Susan Love says that some of the side effects of taking testosterone may include "acne, facial hair, liver disease and weight gain."[26] She also refers to evidence that testosterone may "compound the carcinogenic effect of estrogen on the breast and uterus."[27] As with all hormones, the effects vary hugely from individual to individual.

Testosterone is just one of five androgens, or male-like hormones, in the female body. DHEA is another. You may have seen a lot of information about the antiaging benefits of this hormone—and DHEA supplements for sale in your health food store. But according to Dr. Love, so far, there has been no hard data to support the age-reversing effects of DHEA.[28]

25. Borysenko, Joan, *A Woman's Book of Life*, 148.
26. Love, Susan M., and Lindsey, Karen, *Dr. Susan Love's Hormone Book*, 274.
27. Ibid., 274.
28. Ibid., 274.

Navigating the Choppy Waters
of Hormone Replacement Therapy

Now that you've been officially initiated into the complex world of hormones, you may, like most of us, feel more confused than ever, especially if you're considering (and/or afraid of) taking hormone replacements. How do you know which hormones to take, in what dosages and for how long? As with everything else that goes in or out of balance, you have to experiment.

- All the doctors and specialists I've quoted here follow a natural, conservative and complementary medicine approach to hormone replacement. They agree that you should first try making similar dietary and life-style changes as those outlined in this book. If these don't offer enough relief, keep up these practices and try over-the-counter progesterone cream. If this doesn't help, you may want a prescription for a "natural" estrogen (Estrace, Estraderm and Climara are some brand names. You can also purchase natural hormones through the pharmacies listed in "Resources"). If natural estrogen doesn't offer relief, then you might want to go on the stronger medications, Premarin and Provera.

- A hormone test can help determine which hormones you need or have in excess. Your doctor can administer blood and urine hormone tests. Or you can order a saliva home-test kit, which many doctors believe is more accurate. (See "Resources" for information on these mail-order tests.)

- If you decide to take hormones, start with the lowest possible dosage and, if necessary, increase the dosage gradually, under your doctor's guidance. Likewise, when you stop taking hormones, come off gradually to avoid shocking your system.

- Every one of us has a different genetic background, with various risks for cancer, heart disease and osteoporosis. You should consider these factors when making your decision—your doctor can help you weigh your different risks. For instance, if you're afraid of taking any type of estrogen because it increases your risk for breast cancer yet you have a strong family history of heart disease, you should respect the family history of heart disease more than the cancer. (More than eight times as many women die every year from heart disease than from all types of cancer combined.)[29]

29. Vliet, Elizabeth Lee, *Screaming to Be Heard*, 17.

- One "hormone recipe" may work for you one year but not the next. Stay on top of how you're feeling. You can always change your therapy.

- Hormone replacement doesn't have to be a lifelong venture. You can try it for a few months and if you don't like the results, you can change dosages, medications or stop.

Create Your Own Menstrual Mandala

Throughout our menstrual lives, every month we die a little and are reborn. Darkness and rest are built into our bodies, just as the moon rolls between new and full, as the sun rises and sets and as the earth tilts between spring and fall. Without our menstrual "dark side," there would be no spring, dawn or full moon.

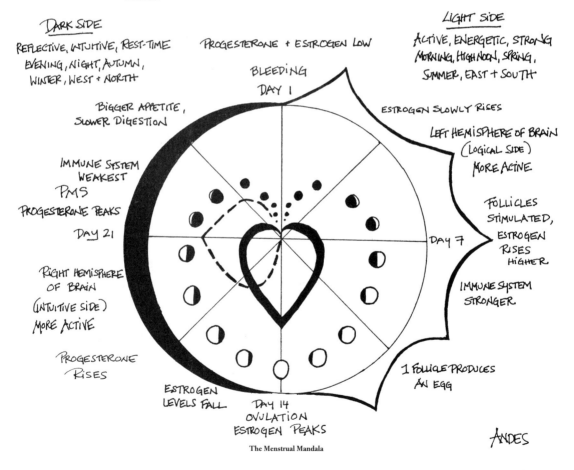

The Menstrual Mandala

To appreciate, make peace with and better understand *your* menstrual cycle, try keeping a "menstrual journal" for several months. Make note of your energy levels, your moods, your downtimes, your sudden energy drops, your cravings, your eating habits, your physical activities, also the effect of medications, drugs and alcohol. Notice the patterns. Are your PMS symptoms worse immediately after ovulation, around day 22 or the day before your period? Or is it different every month? Are your periods easier or harder when you bleed with the full or new moon? Charting your patterns will help you know yourself better, so that you can stay in balance longer and give yourself the types of food, exercise and positive thinking that ease you through your cycle.

When possible, schedule surgeries, big meetings or other times when you're most "out in the world" during the light, "follicular phase" between your period and ovulation. Use the "dark side" of the cycle to process the information that you've received, to rest and weed through your spiritual, intellectual and emotional closet and take true assessments about what you really need or don't. Take a day off when you need it or, if possible, find a group of like-minded women and create a local "moon lodge."

Along the way, take stock of your attitude about your entire "menstrual experience." Who first taught you about menstruation and what beliefs did you acquire which you can now discard? Do you still carry any old "wounds," "dread" or disgust about it? Do you still call it "the curse"? Purge yourself of old negative beliefs and learn to honor how your menstrual life has the power to link you up to your intuition and help you cleanse your body and soul.

While you're cleaning out your old beliefs, ask if you're afraid of menopause. Do you have a list of assumptions and fears of that process? Do you see it as a loss of sexuality and femininity or a time of freedom, power and clear thinking? Are you aware of your particular family's history and the health risks that you might carry—especially after menopause? If you inform yourself about hormones, your risks, and what to do about them, and you fully participate in your well-being instead of being passive in the process and taking whatever medication your doctor prescribes, you'll have a much more positive menopausal transition.

If the spirit moves you, make a map of your monthly cycle (whether still menstruating or not). Do it for several months on end to see any patterns or lack thereof. Turn your findings into a mandala, interpreting the information factually, creatively or both. (Notice the similarity between my Menstrual Mandala and the Movement Mandala. Both are divided into four main quadrants. The Menstrual Mandala's four sections consist of seven days each.) Post your own Menstrual Mandala where you can refer to it often so you can appreciate the beauty of wherever you happen to be on the wheel—and see how it fits into the whole design.

When you see the pattern and artwork embedded in your body's rhythms and arhythms, you learn a new respect for both your shadow and your radiance. Owning your whole self this way, lovingly and without fear or apology, gives you a sense of lasting balance—and supports you in becoming a powerful force in your own life and out in the world.

Goddess of Balance and Bliss

10 Spreading the Way of Balance

The body can provide one of the simplest places to learn the lessons of balance—and also the most humbling. We can experience intellectual or spiritual inspiration in an instant. But physical changes happen one cell, one nerve ending and one muscle fiber at a time. If we try to advance too fast, we get frustrated, get hurt or collapse. Yet if we put aside our movement practice for too long (three to five days is about the max), we start to lose touch; the body-mind connection gets dim. To truly stay in balance, we need to move our bodies mindfully throughout our lives (and eat intelligently and honor our hormonal changes). But when we learn to find bliss at least in movement, it can become one of the most pleasurable parts of our lives!

Most people, I would venture to guess, don't find bliss in movement. Of the 20 to 25 percent of the American population who take *any* regular exercise, most do it to manage stress and body fat and keep muscles, bones and joints strong and healthy—which are all very worthy goals. But where's the joy? To fall in love with movement we have to engage the soul, which, like a child, loves to explore, dance and live out healthy fantasies. It takes one look at a treadmill and folds up its wings unless you let it make up games and play. When the soul is engaged, the body follows and so do the physical benefits.

Working the body and soul on a regular basis in a joyful, exploratory and devotional manner gives us much more than physical rewards. It transports us into deeper parts of ourselves and teaches us that we have the power to transform our bodies, minds, energy, spirits and emotions in an alchemical process, in which we become both the alchemist and the gold. We may not always be able to turn "dark" sensations into light ones or weaknesses into strengths. But we can change our *opinions* and turn "negative" sensations, emotions, experiences or sides of our selves into opportunities for spiritual growth.

For instance, when we tailor a yoga practice to honor PMS, menstruation, menopause or pregnancy, we are practicing compassion with our various hormonal states. Sometimes the postures will bring peace and relief. Sometimes they won't. But using a movement practice to change negative states into positive ones isn't always realistic and isn't the main point. The point is, if we love our "shortcomings" (as much as our strengths) and weave them into our lives and workouts (instead of using them as excuses not to move), we become whole. We'll tend not to carry as many unrealistic expectations to be "up," happy all the time or to have "perfect" bodies or lives. Therefore, we won't feel so disappointed by the reality.

I've found that in my own practice, when I can somehow honor, express or put my vulnerabilities, "failings" and frustrations into whatever form of movement I'm doing, I soften up inside, become real, feel compassion for myself. If I'm sad, I cradle that sadness like a baby as I carefully move. Sometimes the sadness lifts. In the midst of grieving, I have felt my heart swell with mysterious rushes of joy. Other times I allow myself to fully experience the weight and slow speed of sadness without rushing to get it over with. Putting my emotions into physical form this way helps me feel them more profoundly; it expands my self-expression and my understanding of what it means to be human.

My physical practices have probably saved my life—or at least my spirit. I dread to think of what my life would have been like without them. On my mother's side of my family, there's a family history of depression, addiction and cancer. Growing up, I watched relatives and friends of the family drink too much and later die of alcohol-related illnesses. There were suicides. I watched my mother die of colon cancer at age forty-five—an age when otherwise she would have been at the peak of her beauty and power. I often wonder if that cancer would have spread if she'd let herself dance or swim (as she loved to do) on a regular basis and didn't eat so much fatty meat and dairy products. Back then, however, we didn't know much about health. Now we have access to so much information that ignorance is no longer an excuse. This makes it all the more painful these days to watch people self-destruct.

Not too long ago, my childhood best friend died of a drug overdose at age forty-two. She was my dress-up and dance-around-the-room buddy—and the most beautiful child, a strong and natural tumbler, swimmer, diver and dancer. In high school, like a lot of stupid kids, she started taking drugs—but, unlike most of us, never stopped. Several times throughout our adulthood, I tried to get her to dance and swim with me, even tried to entice her into a weight room by informing her that she had the perfect bodybuilder's body type. I thought that if she remembered what a natural dancer and athlete she was, she'd *want* to get sober. But she never made that choice and I couldn't convince her. Our childhood dress-up and dance games gave us both a taste for magic. But, like Alice in Wonderland, she just kept eating from the wrong side of the mushroom.

It took me decades to realize it, but the magic I've been seeking since those days is the kind we brew inside our own bodies. It doesn't come from "out there," from drugs or some elusive mystical power that only favors certain people. Anyone can cultivate it inside with care, practice and imagination.

An interviewer once asked me if people find my approach to movement too spiritual and too serious. Although I'm serious about the benefits of physical practice and advocate serious study, this is not a solemn path. I am truly devoted to movement to have more fun and feel good so that I can express myself fully, embrace life, and let love gush from my heart. When I teach classes, I seldom get the opportunity to talk about the spiritual *inspiration* behind all this movement, because we're so busy moving. Writing gives me the opportunity to describe very private and profound movement experiences. Most athletes, dancers, weight lifters, martial artists, yoginis and others tend to write about the *mechanics* of motion but seldom describe what it *feels* like to move with both mastery and magic. I also wanted to give a voice to the *feminine* sensibility in motion for the women who travel this path.

I have found that "average" women are potentially wonderful movement artists—not because of our strength or speed or degree of fitness, but because of our humility and our desire to create and express ourselves, even if our technique is raw, unpolished. We *want* to play and long to cut the lines that hold our spirits down for at least a few hours a week and float effortlessly like dakinis, high above the gravity of our lives. These mini doses of bliss help us return to the dry, flat planet we sometimes *think* we live in (and even to our houses under construction), with a much better sense of humor and style.

There are a thousand ways to pray and many paths into the temple. Sometimes we surprise ourselves with how quickly we can get there. Improvisation, music, imagination, costumes, ornaments, props, aromatic oils, the right light or even the support of a group all have the power to switch on Shakti energy in an erotic rush. But to have this on a *regular basis* we need to maintain a *solid practice* even during the hard times of our lives. After all, it's during hard times when we need bliss the most.

The movement arts have the power to heal us in profound and personal ways—and we desperately need this sort of healing in our personal lives and in the culture and in the world in general. Disciplined, devotional movement reminds us every day to act compassionately, to start from the beginning and warm up slowly. Over time, the benefits add up and turn our bodies into healthy, expressive and vibrant containers of spirit.

Many years ago, when I began this spiritual journey into movement, I felt somewhat alone. Now, every day I meet another person on this path so I'm assured that our numbers are growing and our influence in the world is getting stronger. We also have more places to play. But there are still plenty of women, plus teenagers and men of all ages, still trying to *beat* themselves into shape or missing out on movement pleasure because it seems boring or hard. I still get frustrated, therefore, because evolution sometimes feels so slow.

I have often asked for guidance about the best way to spread this message. These books have helped me put my beliefs and experiences into words and have secured my dancing feet on this path. But sometimes, guidance tells me to remain silent because one of the *best* ways to inspire others is simply to do the practices and wear the results. Yoginis, dakinis and devadasis, after all, attracted others onto the path not with words but with dances, postures, mudras and quick movements to snap others awake.

Perhaps in a few years or generations, this mindful, balanced approach to movement and life will be considered normal—and imbalanced approaches will look "mindless" and passé. But before that becomes a reality, those of us on this path still must return to the humble act of daily practice. This, after all, is what nourishes us and keeps us in balance. The wise yogini may offer the skull cup of nectar to others at any time, but must first and always take the first sip.

Goddess of Abundance

Resources

Music

We don't just hear music, we *feel* it. As Don Campbell explains in his thought-provoking book *The Mozart Effect,* music stimulates the auditory nerve, which connects to the inner ear, which in turn is connected to every muscle in the body.[1] Campbell says that pleasing music (such as Mozart's intelligent, sweet and well-balanced compositions, with just the right proportions of sound and no sound) has the power to slow and regulate heart rate, lower blood pressure, provide energy and endurance, boost the immune system and stimulate the release of endorphins. It also changes brain waves from the normal beta state into the relaxed alpha state or creatively charged theta state. Music that wears on the nerves, however (like

1. Campbell, Don, *The Mozart Effect: Tapping the Power of Music to Heal the Body, Strengthen the Mind and Unlock the Creative Spirit* (New York: Avon Books, 1997), 68.

heavy metal, rap, grunge, disco or anything *you* think is "noise"), has the opposite effect. "Music" like this raises heart rates and blood pressure (one reason why they play this music in gyms and exercise classes) but it can also weaken the immune system and inspire a release of adrenaline and other stress hormones.[2]

Therefore, since music is a kind of medicine, it should be used wisely. Music is certainly the *dancer's* favorite drug. As a teacher, I take my position as DJ very seriously and understand that music sets the energy for everyone in the room. It should inspire, not interfere with or deaden the nerves. After a dry decade in which I found little music that inspired me (especially that canned disco stuff made for the exercise industry), I'm finally finding music again that makes me want to move! There's a wonderful new batch of "world music," which blends various cultural sounds, ancient and new, into beautiful new rhythms and melodies that stir the soul and move your feet.

The following are my most recent "pick hits," which serve many types of movement. For a CD to make it onto this list, it has to have at least four good cuts or contain twenty minutes of usable music. Some of these CDs are hard to find. To make your search easier, you can order most of the following, and the music listed in *A Woman's Book of Power,* directly through my Web site (**www.worlddancer.com**) or from Backroads Music, described after the CDs.

Afro Celt Sound System, *Volume 1: Sound Magic.* Celtic music has been reinvented and reborn! This is hot dance music, the kind that could blow away the bluest blues on a cold winter's day. Many of the songs take you by surprise. Just when the Uilleann pipes (Irish bagpipes) lull you into mournful complacency, the beat comes on like a freight train and blasts you out of your chair. Favorite cuts: 1, 2, 3, 7.

Robin Adnan Anders, *Omaiyo.* This very diverse collection of sounds combines African, Latin, Balinese, Middle Eastern and R&B. The title cut, "Omaiyo," means "follow the bliss!" A truly uplifting song. Other favorites include Middle Eastern rhythms and mellow Sufi drumming. Favorite cuts: 1, 3, 6, 8.

Anugama, *Shamanic Dream.* This is my favorite yoga or muscle-trance music. Contains two thirty-minute cuts of what Anugama calla "metamusic"—multicultural sounds with mellow rhythms and frequencies designed for relaxation and inner voyaging.

---

2. Ibid., 67.

Anugama and Sebastiano, *Exotic Dance.* This is a teacher's CD. When I want fifteen minutes of solid uninterrupted mod-tempo drumming, especially good for dancing, I reach for this one. It also has a twenty-minute song called "Arabic Journey" that is a bit trancey for my dancing taste but is very good for creating a meditative atmosphere for muscle work. Favorite cut: 1.

James Asher, *Tigers of the Raj.* Normally I don't like electronic music and though I like *some* classical Indian music, much of it gets a little too nasal and arrhythmic for me. However, James Asher blends electronics and Hindu-flavored music in a very compelling way. Some are very danceable, steady rhythms with intricate layers, Middle Eastern flavors and an overlay of jazz. Lovely sitar and vocals, too. Favorite cuts: 1, 4, 5, 6, 9.

Baka Beyond, *Journey Between.* This latest release from Martin Craddock is (like my favorite, *The Meeting Pool*) yet another wonderful combination of Celtic meets Cameroonian pygmies. What an unlikely but happy marriage. Other international influences come from the Hebrides, Bhutan, Ghana, Senegal and Scotland. One cut, described as an "Afro/Breton/Cornish hoe-down," is the only all-out, bust-a-gut dance piece. The rest feature awesome fiddling, beautiful melodies and steady tempos, useful for warm-ups, moderate-paced dances and meditative muscle work. Some beautiful slow pieces for yoga warm-ups and stretching. Favorite cuts: 1, 2, 4, 8.

Big Noise #1, *Funky Tropicalismo!* When I need an upbeat, pull-out-the-stops, infectious dance song, I grab Big Noise, a totally fun combination of African, Latin and jazz, featuring such world musicians and groups as Kanda Bongo Man, Mambomania, Usted Nusrat Fateh Ali Khan, Airto, Ramsey Lewis and the Red Budd Gospel Choir. Favorite cuts: 1, 4, 5, 10, 14 (this last cut will launch you through the roof right into God's arms!).

Don Campbell, *The Mozart Effect.* The companion CDs to Don Campbell's book feature Mozart for medicinal purposes. Volume 1 is "Strengthen the Mind." Volume 2 is "Heal the Body" (refreshing yoga music—a nice change from New Age music that all sounds the same). Volume 3 is "Music for Creativity and Imagination." He also has Mozart CDs for kids: Volume 1 is "Tune Up Your Mind." Volume 2 is "Relax, Daydream and Draw." Volume 3 is "Mozart in Motion." It's all good. You can't go wrong with Mozart.

Delerium, *Karma.* Intensely danceable, steady tempos. Many start with slow, luscious openings and then break open into full dance music. A very playful and original combination of sounds: African, Flamenco, chanting monks, tar drum, sitar and a little electronic rock and roll. Most songs can be used for warm-ups, dancing, muscle or floor work. Favorite cuts: 1, 4, 6(!!!), 8, 9, 10.

Jim Donovan, *Indigo.* This is an unusual CD. I pull it out when I'm teaching very focused, precise muscle work or yoga and don't want an invasive heavy beat stealing people's attention. I wouldn't play this at a party or in a dance class. But this CD provides a very useful "color" in my "palette" of music styles. Hypnotic, repetitive, slightly annoying if you listen to it too closely but perfect for teaching. Favorite cut: there's only one sixty-minute track of uninterrupted music!

Robert Gass, *Alleluia/Kyrie* and *Om Namaha Shivaya.* These beautifully simple chants are perfect for dancing or doing yoga *while chanting* (a wonderful internal and external exercise!). The Alleluia is sung to Pachelbel's Canon. The Om Nama Shiva is an endless loop of ecstatic chanting. His new CD *Enchanted: The Best of Robert Gass and Wings of Song* is available from Spring Hill Music, Box 800, Boulder, CO 80306-0800; Phone: 303-938-1188; Fax: 303-938-1191; E-mail: netcomm@springhillmedia.com; Website: www.springhillmedia.com. I also recommend Robert Gass's book, *Chanting: Discovering Spirit in Sound* (New York: Broadway Books, 1999).

Jim McGrath, *Soul Dancer.* Sixty-six minutes of solid drumming. Some of it is steady and great for teaching and some of it gets into complicated rhythms that are a bit more challenging to move to in a group (you have to wait for the beat to come back to you). All in all, a good investment for a movement teacher. Favorite cuts: 1, 2, 4.

Loreena McKennitt, *The Book of Secrets.* Loreena is my music goddess. Her sounds come from an ancient world that I'd like to live in, at least part of the time. Every corpuscle in my body responds to Loreena's Celtic and Middle Eastern combinations. I have also performed to about four different Loreena songs, perhaps because she switches with such grace from devotional to all-out dance music. You can warm up, dance yourself into a froth, do muscle work and yoga and end in prayer with this CD. Favorite cuts: 1, 2, 4, 6, 8.

Professor Trance, *Medicine Trance.* This has to be my all-time favorite teaching CD. This two-CD set contains only six cuts—and not one of them is shorter than twenty minutes. All are steady, rhythmic, trance-inducing and useful for dancing or muscle work. Not as "heavy" as Professor Trance's first CD, *Shaman's Breath*. Favorite cuts: all!

Hossam Ramzy, *Baladi Plus: Egyptian Dance Music.* Great music for tribal-style belly dance. Very steady, danceable Baladi rhythms everyone can dance to, some snaky and luscious slow music and playful, always-changing rhythms, fun for performing or dancing games. Favorite cuts: 1, 2, 3, 6, 8.

Suhaila Salimpour, *Rhythmic Journey.* (Available through Suhaila at 510-526-4344 or www.suhaila.com). Suhaila is a famous Bay Area belly dancing goddess. This CD features a twenty-two minute drum solo that can lift you up and keep you there for a long time. Favorite cut: 4.

Paul Schwartz and Mario Grigorov, *Aria.* This is one of the few dance CDs I can listen to while I write. An incredibly creative combination of famous operatic arias, rhythm and jazz. The female sopranos are awesome and inspire lyrical, passionate moves. Favorite cuts: 2 (*Madame Butterfly*), 3, 7 (*Carmen!*).

Vas, *Sunyata.* This is a winner. The beautiful female vocalist, Azim Ali, was born in Iran, educated in India, schooled in Persian classical music and, combining those influences, sings in a haunting language all her own. Her partner, Greg Ellis, plays impressive percussion. Their combined talents add up to over an hour's worth of dancing, muscle or yoga bliss from upbeat into lyrical into stillness supreme. Favorite cuts: 1, 4, 6, 7, 9, 10.

Vas, *Offerings.* This second release seems even more devotional than the first (if that's possible). Azim Ali's voice is perfect for more inner journeying through dance, yoga or strength moves. Many songs have slow, luscious introductions followed by upbeat rhythms plus lyrical Persian–Middle Eastern melodies. Favorite cuts: 1, 4, 7, 9.

Willie and Lobo, *Caliente.* I can't decide which I love more about these guys—their music or their faces. These ex-patriot surfers with wonderful craggy mugs play an incredibly delicate combination of flamenco and Moorish music. They also seem to draw divine inspiration from the sun and sea in Puerto Vallarta, Mexico. Favorite cuts: 1, 3, 5, 10.

One of my favorite sources for music is **Backroads Music.** This catalogue and music fulfillment company (not a store) serves up an impressive selection of these and other great underground hits. You can also call them up and say, "I need some massage music with a Celtic sound" or "I need some rhythmic dance music with a Hindu flavor," and they'll oblige with more CD suggestions than you can believe. If you live in the San Francisco Bay Area (they're in Marin), you can drop by and listen to music for hours without seeming to get in their way. They've turned me on to so many great sounds, I'm indebted to them. Backroads Music is at 418 Tamal Plaza, Corte Madera, CA 94925. 1-800-767-4748. Fax: 1-415-924-0648. Web site: www.backroadsmusic.com

Videos

After too many years writing books about movement and teaching, I finally have a video to go along with these books. *The WomanPower Workout* is a cocreation with Carolena Nericcio (founder of FatChanceBellyDance, featured in *A Woman's Book of Power*, also a teacher, dancing goddess and business-woman extraordinaire). The first section of this video features my warm-up with easy flow-dancing, graceful yet potent leg work and a vigorous veil dance. The second section features Carolena's American tribal-style belly dance in a simple, follow-along format. The third section contains fifteen minutes of strength training using the pole and band or dumbbells. The cool-down features the Temple Dance form described in this book. In this valid and varied workout, you get fifty minutes of moderate, fun, "fat-burning" moves that celebrate your beauty and womanly body, and kinesthetically intelligent exercises for strength, flexibility and movement bliss.

To order this and other videos, please visit our Web sites at www.world-dancer.com and www.fcbd.com.

Equipment

You can create your pole and band combo in a variety of ways. The bands, called P.R.O. bands (Progressive Resistance with Options), are five feet, four inches long and have loops on the ends (through which you slide the pole). I find that the medium-strength bands (green) seem to work well for most women.

The P.R.O. bars (featured in this book) are padded, lightweight wooden dowels covered with soft foam padding. However, you have many options when it comes to poles. Both Carolena Nericcio of FatChanceBellyDance and I sell the break-apart poles and bands with our *WomanPower Workout* video. The break-apart pole is about three feet long and breaks into two pieces that fit neatly in most suitcases. (See our Web site addresses above.)

If traveling with your pole isn't important, you can also make your own pole. Buy a four-foot-long closet dowel in a hardware store. Put 1 1/4" rubber furniture bumpers on the ends to protect your wooden floors from scratches.

P.R.O. bands and P.R.O. bars (in break-apart or non-break-apart versions) are also available from Fitness Wholesale. Call 1-888-FW-ORDER or visit www.fitnesswholesale.com.

Yoga

If you're going to do yoga on a wooden floor, you should have a sticky mat so you can hold the postures without slipping. For a sticky mat (basic or deluxe) and a whole host of yoga props (blocks, foam, belts, bolsters, blankets, balls, books and videos), contact: Hugger Mugger Yoga Products, 1-800-473-4888 (M–F, 9:30 to 5:30 Mountain time); fax 801-487-4898 or visit www.yogacentral.com/hugger. Hugger Mugger mats are also available through Fitness Wholesale (see above).

Food

Chai. You can find many brands of chai in health food stores, some coffee stores and big chain stores like Trader Joe's. My favorite brand is Oregon Chai. It's sweet, spicy and not as expensive as other brands and the box is full of irreverent humor. To find out who sells it in your area call 1-888-874-CHAI (2424).

Tasty soy products—meat alternatives. The only way some men will eat soy is if it tastes like meat, and Yves' products pass the test. Yves' Veggie Cuisine has some tasty, fat-free Canadian Veggie Bacon (delicious sautéed and sliced up in a rice or tabouli salad), Veggie Ground Round and Sausages. There are also several varieties of burgers, hot dogs, and other products. Visit Yves' Web site at www.yvesveggie.com for information on products, recipes and stores in your area (in the United States and Canada) that carry these products.

Hormones

Hormone testing. Aeron Life Cycles makes an easy in-home hormone test that can determine if your hormone levels are within the normal range for your age. This saliva test measures circulating levels of hormones and is thought to be more accurate than blood tests. (Hormone levels in saliva stay stable at room temperature for a long time so you don't have to ship your sample under refrigeration.) Tests can measure the levels of one or more of these hormones: estradiol, progesterone, testosterone, DHEA and melatonin (which regulates sleep rhythms). The price per test is $49.50 for one hormone, $86.70 for two, $123.80 for three and $154.60 for four. Prices don't include shipping or California state sales tax. Medical insurance *doesn't* cover the price of the test. Results are sent to your medical provider for interpretation. For more information on the test kits (Aeron also sells progesterone creams), phone 1-800-631-7900; fax 510-729-0383 or visit their Web site at www.aeron.com. Their mailing address is 1933 Davis St., Ste. 310, San Leandro, CA 94577. Don't forget to read their information concerning the best times of the day and month to collect saliva.

Pharmacies for natural hormones. Two well-known, long-established pharmacies specialize in filling individualized prescriptions for natural hormones. Both also offer education and consultations on PMS and menopause.

Madison Pharmacy in Madison, WI (Marla Ahlgrimm, R.Ph. [registered pharmacist], founder and president). You can schedule a ten-minute phone conversation with a registered pharmacist to see if natural hormones are right for you (cost, $2.00 a minute). Call them at 1-800-558-7046 or visit their Web site at www.womenshealth.com. Madison Pharmacy is also associated with Aeron Life Cycles.

Belmar Pharmacy in Lakewood, CO (Charles Hakala, R.Ph.). Belmar creates not only hormones but also a line of vitamins tailored for various women's needs. They use no dyes or milk products and so all formulas are hypoallergenic. Call them at 1-800-525-9473 or visit their Web site at www.belmarpharmacy.com.

Return to the Temple

I dream myself back to the temple,
To my passion, my calling, my home.
Shoeless on a warm stone floor,
Feet pound heavenly rhythms
And agile, anxious fingers
Pluck stories from the air
All to dance your praises.

I swim back to the temple,
Cross two oceans, three continents and
Lifetimes in cold places
To serve, worship and adore you.
Nothing can hold me back from you and
This temple of my beginnings.

Oh to be bathed like a bride,
Sanctified with sandalwood paste,
Dotted with the holy dazzle between my brows,
Perfumed, prayed for and initiated once again
As a devadasi in your service.

For you, I hang my nightgown on a hook,
Leave the car keys on the table,
A note on the microwave that says,
"Gone out for a while, honey. Not sure when I'll be back"
And rise up the chimney in a curl of smoke,
To spin and drift my way back to you,
My deity lover.

I am soaring above the temple,
Unburdened, naked and free,
Flying over pointed spires piercing clouds of dust,
Where goat bells clang beneath me
And curries boil over open flames.
What clarity befell me?
What memory weeded up
Through so many empty lives and broken homes
And brought me back to you?

In a breath I am back in the temple
Where little has changed in two thousand years.
As if I did this yesterday,
I lay flowers at your altar,
Prepare your plate of chutney and rice,
Rub your lingam with oils,
And devote myself to you completely—
So much easier than with a real man.

I am dancing once again in the temple, starting on my knees.
Epics, stored for centuries,
Spill from my fingertips.
Jewels drip from every flash of skin.
You do not ask "are you going out dressed like that?"

Instead you twinkle your praises in my bracelets and bells.
"Dance with me now" you say
And so I become this moment, this beating heart and radiant power,
With no greater ambition than this.

We are dancing in duet, you and me,
Waltzing through the heart of the temple,
Moving into melting bliss.
Your fire licks my backbone.
Your wisdom sneaks across my smiling face
I am brazen, humble, passionate and shy
Because you dance inside me.

I sleep inside the temple,
Curled around your image with the other dancers who praise you.
Sprawled on silken pillows and under a woven sheet,
Nursing our bodies with food, oils and songs of praise,
We rest, so that we may dance this way for years,
And devote our rhythmic lives to you.

I dream inside the temple,
Of a handsome man on a tree-lined street,
Searching for his dinner, his Shakti and his smile.
Swells of yearning tug at my womb and mortal desires.
Yet that world feels so distant now
Where the people, so disconnected,
Search for the wrong types of bliss.

Here inside the temple,
I have tasted your ecstasy
And buried my history in a rosewood box
Under sandy soil and a layer of tears
To cut away the past and serve you.

"But this is not where you are needed," you say.
And though I try not to listen,
The world I left behind cries for my return.
"Let me stay a little longer," I beg of you

And you soften into a breeze that
Ruffles my silk, penetrates my pores and evaporates my tears.
I know I must leave the temple.
"But you can take me with you," you say.
"I'll always be dancing inside."

—Karen Andes

Bibliography

Argüelles, José and Miriam. *Mandala*. Boston and London: Shambhala, 1995.

Avtar, Ram. *Indian Dances: History and Development*. New Delhi, India: Pankaj Publications, 1984.

Barlow, Bernice. *Sacred Sites of the West*. St. Paul, MN: Llewellyn Publications, 1996.

Bernhardt, Patrick. *The Secret Music of the Soul*. Quebec, Canada: Imagine Books and Records, 1991.

Bonheim, Jalaja. *Aphrodite's Daughters: Women's Sexual Stories and the Journey of the Soul*. New York: Simon & Schuster, 1997.

Borysenko, Joan, Ph.D. *A Woman's Book of Life: The Biology, Psychology, and Spirituality of the Feminine Life Cycle*. New York: Riverhead Books, 1997.

Campbell, Don. *The Mozart Effect: Tapping the Power of Music to Heal the Body, Strengthen the Mind and Unlock the Creative Spirit*. New York: Avon Books, 1997.

Cornell, Judith. *Mandala: Luminous Symbols for Healing*. Wheaton, IL: Quest Books, 1994.

Cruden, Loren. *The Spirit of Place: A Workbook for Sacred Alignment*. Rochester, VT, Destiny Books, 1995.

Devi, Ragini. *Dance Dialects of India*. Delhi, India: Shri Jainendra Press, 1972; 2nd edition, 1990.

Doczi, George. *The Power of Limits: Proportional Harmonies in Nature, Art and Architecture*. Boston and London: Shambhala, 1994.

Frawley, David. *Tantric Yoga and the Wisdom Goddesses*. Salt Lake City, UT: Morson, 1994.

Gass, Robert. *Chanting: Discovering Spirit in Sound*. New York: Broadway Books, 1999.

Heselton, Philip. *Earth Mysteries*. Dorset, England, and Rockport, MA: Element Books, 1995.

Jung, C. G. *Mandala Symbolism*. Princeton, NJ: Bollingen Series, Princeton University Press, 1959.

Kishore, B. R. *Dances of India*. New Delhi, India: Diamond Pocket Books, 1988.

Kryder, Rowena Patte. *Sacred Ground to Sacred Space: Visionary Ecology, Perennial Wisdom, Environmental Ritual and Art*. Santa Fe, NM: Bear and Company, 1994.

Lark, Susan. *Women's Health Companion: Self-Help Nutrition Guide and Cookbook*. Berkeley, CA: Celestial Arts, 1996.

Lawlor, Robert. *Sacred Geometry, Philosophy and Practice*. London: Thames and Hudson, 1982.

Leidy, Denise Patry, and Thurman, Robert. *Mandala: The Architecture of Enlightenment*. New York: Asia Society Galleries and Tibet House, 1997.

Leonard, George, and Murphy, Michael. *The Life We Are Given: A Long-Term Program for Realizing the Potential of Body, Mind, Heart and Soul*. New York: J. P. Tarcher/Putnam, 1995.

Love, Susan M., M.D., and Lindsey, Karen. *Dr. Susan Love's Hormone Book*. New York: Random House, 1997.

Mann, A. T. *Sacred Architecture*. Dorset, England: Element Books, 1993.

Northrup, Christiane, M.D. *Women's Bodies, Women's Wisdom*. New York: Bantam Doubleday, 2nd edition, 1998.

Robinson, Lynne, and Thomson, Gordon. *Body Control the Pilates Way*. London: Newleaf, 1997.

Rossbach, Sarah. *Interior Design with Feng Shui*. New York: Penguin, 1987.

Roth, Gabrielle. *Sweat Your Prayers: Movement as a Spiritual Practice.* New York: J. P. Tarcher/Putnam, 1997.

Sarabhai, Mrinalini. *Understanding Bharata Natyam.* Gujarat, India: Darpana Publications, 1996.

Schneider, Michael S. *A Beginner's Guide to Constructing the Universe: The Mathematical Archetypes of Nature, Art and Science.* New York: Harper Perennial, 1994.

Schwab, Roger. *Strength of a Woman: The Truth about Training the Female Body.* Bryn Mawr, PA: Main Line Publications, 1997.

Shaw, Miranda. *Passionate Enlightenment: Women in Tantric Buddhism.* Princeton, NJ: Princeton University Press, 1994.

Sheehy, Gail. *The Silent Passage.* New York: Random House, 1991.

Snow, Kimberly. *Keys to the Open Gate: A Woman's Spirituality Sourcebook.* Emeryville, CA: Conari Press, 1994.

Vliet, Elizabeth Lee, M.D. *Screaming to Be Heard: Hormonal Connections Women Suspect and Doctors Ignore.* New York: M. Evans and Company, 1995.

Weil, Andrew, M.D. *Natural Health, Natural Medicine.* Boston: Houghton Mifflin, 1995.

Wosien, Maria Gabriele. *Sacred Dance: Encounters with Gods.* New York: Avon Books, 1974.

Ywahoo, Dhyani. *Voices of Our Ancestors: Cherokee Teachings from the Wisdom Fire.* Boston: Shambhala, 1987.

Index

ABOUT THE AUTHOR

Karen Andes is the author of several books, a teacher, video producer, public speaker, sacred dancer, yogini, cyber gal, personal trainer, businesswoman and pilgrim on the path. Ms. Andes lives in "the temple" she and her husband are building in San Rafael, California.

TO CONTACT KAREN ANDES

To find out more information about Karen's other books, videos, classes, personal training sessions or to invite her to participate in your event, visit her Web site at: www.worlddancer.com

Send E-mail to kandes@worlddancer.com

Send letters to Karen Andes
c/o Penguin Putnam Inc.
375 Hudson Street
New York, New York 10014